Project You
A Manual Of
Rational
Assertiveness
Training

By Claudine Paris & Bill Casey
Foreword by Michael J. Mahoney
Cover Design by Susan Ficca

Distributed by

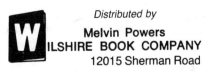

Melvin Powers
ILSHIRE BOOK COMPANY
12015 Sherman Road
No. Hollywood, California 91605
Telephone: (213) 875-1711 / (818) 983-1105

Bridges Press, 615 East 10th Avenue, Suite 12, Denver, CO 80203

International Standard Book Number: 0-87980-408-4

Library of Congress Catalog Card Number: 78-66974

Printed in the United States of America.

Distributed by Wilshire Book Company
12015 Sherman Road, North Hollywood, Calif 91605-3781

CONTENTS

FOREWORD

There are now over a dozen different manuals on assertiveness training and — not surprisingly — most assert that they are very effective. Controlled experimental evaluations of the effectiveness of these manuals is something which will take years to complete. In the meantime, we must base our confidence on the content of these manuals. To the extent that they reflect the current state of knowledge, we may be optimistic about their relevance for personal development. In the case of *Project: You,* I think we are warranted in such optimism.

This is a manual which is written in simple, straight-forward language, and it is filled with many illustrative examples. Besides being easy to read, it covers a wide range of techniques now popular among psychologists. Along with a basic introduction to the concepts of reward and punishment, there is discussion of personal measurement, goal-setting, and even the role of your family and friends in successful self-management. Finally, this manual emphasizes a cognitive-behavioral approach by integrating patterns of thought, feeling, and action. This represents a timely and valuable integration which should enhance the relevance of *Project: You* for your personal efforts.

Claudine Paris and Bill Casey have, in my opinion, brought together a wealth of theoretical knowledge and technical expertise in a very readable and meaningful manner. I have enjoyed reading the manual — when I was assertive enough to get it back from my friends.

Michael J. Mahoney

PREFACE

On Assertiveness Training

Assertiveness training was originally developed by behavioral psychologists. It is, in fact, the only major behavioral technique with its own philosophy: that people should be assertive.

However, people without behavioral training presently lead many assertiveness groups. Their techniques may work; but, since the techniques have not been researched, we have chosen not to include them in *Project: You*.

We have purposely shied away from the language of psychologists. However, the exercises we outline in this manual are all well researched, or based on research, to give you the results you're looking for: a more assertive you!

Furthermore, we see assertion as something positive, rather than a way to get back at the world. While expression of negative feelings may be hard for some, so too, is the expression of positive feelings. We think it's healthy to do **both**. Throughout the book, we have tried to emphasize that the ability to express the negative is founded on the ability to express the positive.

On Rational Assertiveness Training

In the summer of 1973, my wife, Claudine Paris, worked with Drs. Heiner and Marianne Kunze on something called "assertiveness training." Claudine assisted these two psychiatrists in writing and adapting the new technique, which they had learned at the Max Planck Institute in Munich.* When Marianne and Heiner returned to Germany, Claudine continued to use these methods — first with mental health outclients, and later with college students in Denver.

At the same time, I was working with Dr. Rian McMullin on some new cognitive techniques. They were based primarily on social learning theory and Albert Ellis' "rational emotive therapy." Rian had some astute insights as to how these two schools might be combined. We eventually systematized these ideas into a therapy called "cognitive restructuring therapy."

As Claudine and I shared our enthusiasm (and data!) with each other, an idea emerged: why not work on assertive **behavior** and assertive **cognitions** at the same time? After combining the two techniques, we looked at our results. On the various dimensions we were measuring (fears, anxiety, assertiveness, depression), we found between 50% and 100% improvement over the older "straight" assertiveness training. Out of deference to Dr. Ellis — and because we liked the acronym — we called it "Rational Assertiveness Training."

We later wrote a small manual called *Rational Assertiveness Training,* which was the forerunner of this manual. Much has been clarified, and several techniques and concepts have been added. We still believe that the classroom is the best setting for this material, but we have often seen the motivated individual make tremendous changes even without the supervision and group reinforcement. In either case, we believe that the earnest use of this manual can give you a new power over yourself which will have a profoundly positive effect on your life.

Bill Casey

*It is interesting that our involvement in assertiveness training should come by way of Germany, since this is primarily an American development.

CHAPTER 1

ASSERTIVENESS

What is Assertiveness?

There are assertive, aggressive and passive ways of responding to others and ourselves. Since assertiveness is usually confused with aggression, let's straighten that out first.

When we are aggressive we usually get our way. Unfortunately that success may involve a total disregard for others. We may try to make others feel stupid for having an opinion that differs from ours, and we may get angry and yell when others do not comply with our wishes. Or we may use quiet intimidation as a tactic. Aggression is often seen as the only way for people to meet their needs. Such a viewpoint is not only impractical but quite unrealistic as well!

When we act as though our feelings and needs are less important than those of others, we are committing the opposite error: passivity. Although you are the most important person you will ever know, passivity implies just the opposite. The passive person has little visible love for himself. Instead of standing up for himself he takes total responsibility for other people's possible reactions and emotions. "He might be unhappy if I disagree with him." "She'll be disappointed if I don't do what she wants." It's not clear whether they're mind-readers or fortune tellers, but passive people frequently get into the habit of second-guessing the emotions of others. Furthermore, passivity is often a subtle put-down: "I know he can't handle my true feelings, so I'll just be quiet." Or, "She could never stand it if I refused her, so I'd better give in for her sake."

I* see assertiveness as that happy medium between aggressiveness and passivity. In their excellent book *Your Perfect Right*, Alberti and Emmons (1974) define assertive behavior as "behavior which enables a person to act in his own best interest, to stand up for himself without undue anxiety, to express his honest feelings comfortably, or to exercise his own rights without denying the rights of others."

Who Needs It?

People are often labeled as being either "passive," "assertive,"

*The authors will use the word "I" to mean both of them, except where the context clearly indicates which is writing the passage.

or "aggressive." While these labels are neat, simple categorizations, they are inaccurate and misleading. Most people have all these behaviors to varying degrees.

People do not fit into niches very easily. Instead of finding a label for yourself, describe the behaviors you have, and the behaviors you want.

Someone might say, for instance, "My work-related behaviors are usually aggressive and my home-related behaviors are usually passive. I would like to be more assertive."

In the areas where you are passive you have a lot to gain by learning to be assertive. You will learn to stand up for your rights, assert your opinions and make your desires known. As you make your desires known you improve your chances of getting them met. Although you will not get everything you want, you will be getting a lot more in those situations than you got by being passive.

In those areas where you are aggressive, you will have to learn how to extend rights to others. As you recognize the rights of others you will find that: 1) they will be more honest with you; 2) they'll be less likely to respond to you with aggression; 3) there will no longer be that wake of resentment which formerly followed your acts of aggression; and 4) others will respond to you by *choice*, not command.

Perhaps you will notice that it is easier to be assertive with those with whom you are not close. That is not at all unusual. People often find it difficult to be assertive in close relationships. Some of our students have surprised their friends and family by coming to Assertiveness Training class. Others thought they were already as assertive as they needed to be. In some cases our student was labeled as being "too assertive" (usually this means aggressive) Although others may say you are already "assertive enough," only you really know that you fail to be assertive at times. No one else knows when you think something and don't say it. Only you know when you go along with the crowd to avoid criticism. And, you are the only one who knows your behaviors in *all* situations.

You will have to be the judge of whether learning to be more assertive would benefit you. (If you are letting others make the decisions for you, then there is no doubt you need to learn to be assertive.) If you don't have enough information to make the decision, then read on and find out more about it.

2

CHAPTER 2

GETTING READY

The World Is Not the Way It Should Be

Knowing that the world is not the way it should be before you begin is a great timesaver. You no longer need to sit around and lament that "people are not fair," "others do not understand," "people never do things right," "people nowadays do not have the scruples and morals they should have," "everyone always takes advantage of me," or "it is impossible to be happy in such a hectic, uncaring world."

All these statements are a waste of time. They change nothing and promote a feeling of helplessness. They may reflect the assumption that "my beliefs are right and theirs are wrong!" That may be so, but to *expect* people to behave the way they "should" is foolish.

One time I was lamenting the condition of the world. Something had happened at work that I didn't like and I complained to a friend that, "It's just not fair!" He was stunned, and said, "Fair? You expect the world to be fair?" "Right," said I. "Then," he replied, "why don't you go to Heaven! That's the only place you are going to find what you're looking for." That may not be exactly true, but it is a more accurate view of reality than my expectation that all should be fair.

You are setting yourself up for disappointment when you expect others to behave according to your desires. For one thing, the person has the right to act in accordance with his own desires, which may differ from yours. There is always more than one right way to approach something, and you would do well to recognize that in the beginning.

When my kids were around eight and nine, they started to be untidy around the house. Until then they had generally met my expectations of neatness. For a while, I continued to insist on my standards of neatness, then it occurred to me that they had rights, too. So we made a deal. They would be neater about the areas of the house we all shared — the living room, kitchen, etc., — but they would keep their own rooms in whatever state they desired as long as they kept their doors closed. That worked well; we all got what we wanted.

Often your own behaviors will not conform to the desires and expectations of others. That doesn't mean that you are bad or stupid — or that they are! Let's say that you ask your mother to stop calling your apartment at 7:30 every morning. She responds by saying it is not nice for children to criticize their parents. She is neither right nor wrong. She is expressing what she believes; you do not have to agree.

Others may be subtle in trying to get you to "see it my way." They will tell you what you are doing is wrong, destructive or somehow harmful to yourself as well as to others. These accusations are generally cited for the purpose of making you feel uncomfortable with the changes you are making. Listen and evaluate, but do not accept what they say without questioning the validity of their words.

The more passive a person is, the more likely she or he is to attempt to meet the expectations of everybody. Simple decisions become difficult because there is the constant fear that whatever the decision, it will not be given the approval of others. Decisions about which article of clothing to buy, which movie to suggest, or even whether to make a suggestion, become agonizing. What if you buy something and no one likes it? What if everyone thinks the movie you suggest is dumb? Well, nothing. It simply means they have opinions which differ from yours.

You cannot live inside someone else's head, nor they in yours. You will have to act in accordance with your own belief system and give others the right to do the same.

If you've been trying to please everyone, you already know it doesn't work. No matter how hard you try, there are times someone does not like what you do. That being the case, you might as well do what *you* think best; you'll end up with the same results — not everyone will approve. You come out ahead, though, because you acted in accordance with your own beliefs and *you* like what you did.

How Not to Succeed

My most successful students are the people who work very hard to learn from the course and use the book. Interestingly, there is a very high correlation between the amount of time spent on homework, and how much the course is enjoyed.

I sometimes deal with grumbling students, the ones who say, "I don't have time to do the homework." When these

4

students are persuaded to spend an hour per week on homework, they often become ardent supporters!

In addition to "I don't have time," there are some other attitudes which will interfere with your success. I call these attitudes "sabotages." Some are listed below, but there are plenty more.

"This isn't the real me."

The "real you" is a growing, changing human being. Whenever you learn something, the "real you" changes a little. This is true of becoming assertive. You will learn new, more successful ways of dealing with yourself and with others. And isn't that what the "real you" wants?

"The change feels unnatural."

Most changes feel unnatural. For instance, if we were to drive in England, it would feel uncomfortable at first. After all, it's "unnatural" to drive on the left side of the road. Nevertheless, that's a change we would soon grow comfortable with — or else!

When you make significant changes in your life, some discomfort is experienced. That discomfort is used either as an excuse to sabotage your efforts or as a signal that you are successfully battling an old habit.

Changing our thought and behavior habits with regard to assertion is no different. If you are in the habit of letting people walk on you it will seem quite unnatural to start standing up for your rights. If you are in the habit of downgrading yourself, positive self-statements will seem quite unnatural.

"I'm quite willing to listen, but there's no point in 100% commitment."

The old adage, "You only get what you put into it" couldn't be truer here. Half-hearted participation will result in half-baked success.

"I know this isn't going to work."

I could present reams of data and hundreds of testimonials. But that won't do the job. You will simply have to give this a sincere effort, and you will be rewarded with all the evidence you could ask for.

"I'm too far gone for this to work on me."

Such prophecies are always self-fulfilling. As long as you believe your goals are unattainable, they will be. (The prophecy "It will work for me," can also be self-fulfilling.)

People who moan about insoluble personal problems too often spend 90% of the time talking about their problems and 10% working on them. Don't fall into this trap. Even though it's dramatic and interesting to have insurmountable problems, you'll find that with sincere effort you will soon need a new topic of conversation; the problems will be gone!

"Others may not approve of my goals."

Sometimes your goals will not receive the immediate approval of others. If you wait for approval you may be stymied. You cannot go beyond where you are willing to put up with a little flak. If you have been under others' influence to the point that you do only what they want, they are not suddenly going to release you from that control. You will have to work to get your own control.

Patty, one of my students, set a goal to go back to work. She was happy when she was working, but felt dull when she didn't. That seemed like an excellent goal for Patty. Then she said she would let us know for sure next week whether she would definitely have that for a goal. We later learned that she wanted to ask her husband whether it was okay for her to have that goal! No matter how much she wanted to return to work, she was willing to give up that notion if her husband did not immediately agree to it.

"Things haven't worked too well so far, so I'll give up."

Being assertive is just like any other skill. You get better with practice. Naturally you can expect to make a mistake now and then. But what do you expect? This stuff is good, but it isn't magic!

"I've tried everything."

Really? Or have you just "exposed" yourself to everything. Self-help books, group therapy, encounter groups or courses on personal growth don't magically change you. You must put forth some effort in making the changes you desire or those changes don't happen.

6

Doing vs. Wishing

When you are *doing*, you are active. When you are *wishing*, you are passive. It is easier to *wish*, more effective to *do*.

Think of it as being assertive with yourself. Being assertive with yourself means doing; you work on overcoming self-defeating behaviors. Instead of wishing you could lose ten pounds, you actually begin a program to change your eating habits. Instead of wishing you had something to do, you make plans to get involved in an activity you enjoy. Instead of wishing you were more assertive, you carry out the assignments recommended here.

When you get depressed, anxious, fatigued or nervous, look at your life and see what you can do differently. Don't just *wish* for things to improve. Plan a course of action and pursue it.

When you begin to take charge of yourself, to be responsible for yourself, you are taking an active role in shaping your own life.

CHAPTER 3

TEN ASSERTIVE BEHAVIORS

Becoming More Assertive

Once you have determined that you want to "be more assertive," the very next issues to be dealt with are: 1) *what* to do, and 2) *how* to do it. I can help you with both the what and the how, but, first . . .

Assertiveness is a group of behaviors you can learn. The more you practice, the better you will get. The more often you act assertively, the easier it will become.

View assertiveness as a cluster of skills. Expect to have all the same difficulties learning these new skills as with any others. When you first begin to use a new skill you are not as competent as you are after you have had lots of practice. Sometimes in being assertive you will make mistakes. There will be times you forget to use your assertion skills. But as with other skills, practice will pay off.

Following is a list of behaviors that are generally considered assertive. These behaviors are the "what to do's" to become more assertive. They are the road map you can follow. When you have improved in all 10 areas, the new assertive you has begun to emerge!

1. Think and talk about yourself in a positive way.
2. Feel comfortable expressing honest compliments.
3. Accept compliments without embarrassment.
4. Express yourself directly and spontaneously.
   A. Express the positive.
   B. Touch on the "touchy."
5. Ask for what you want.
6. State honest disagreements with ease.
7. Be able to say "no."
8. Insist on fair treatment.
9. Keep in touch with friends.
10. Take the first step in forming new friendships.

The first behaviors are not necessarily the easiest. They are, however, a firm foundation. It is the same principle as building a house from the bottom up. First you establish a firm foundation, then build on that.

Maybe you noticed that behaviors 1, 2, 3 and 4A are all

positive. I call these an environmental cleanup project. As you work on these first four behaviors, you teach yourself to scan for the good things that occur. There are several reasons for wanting you to start out improving positive behaviors. The most important reason is *I want you to succeed.* Your environment accepts changes much better in this direction. Hence, this improves your chances of receiving encouragement for your changes.

Others will not feel threatened by increases in positive behaviors. As you learn to appreciate yourself and your environment you begin to feel happier. This is not likely to upset anyone. Indeed, you will be strengthening relationships, and that will make the going easier when you reach the more advanced behaviors.

Also, "problems" disappear. When you scan for problems, you find them. When you scan for something pleasant, you find that. The more positive you are the fewer problems you find. This is not to suggest you go about wearing your good pair of rose-colored glasses. However, I do suggest that you take a hard and honest look at the positive side.

It is sometimes better to work on new behaviors in "low risk" relationships. These relationships are with people not especially close to you. An acquaintance, a person with whom you do business, or any other person with whom you associate on a fairly uninvolved level. "High risk" relationships, then, are with people you are close to — your family, dear friends and other individuals with whom you are emotionally involved.

Sometimes I will recommend to you that you start working on the new behavior in a low risk relationship. Other times you may decide for yourself that it would be wiser to start off in a low risk relationship.

Following each of the ten assertive behaviors is a list called "Small Beginnings." This is a list of behaviors you may want to try as you are working toward your assertiveness goals.

1. Think and Talk about Yourself in a Positive Way

Our culture has taught us all that it isn't nice to toot your own horn. However, I disagree with that notion. I believe that, just like charity, love begins at home.

It is as though we have been so conditioned not to "brag"

that even *thinking* nice things about ourselves seems wrong. But don't worry — no one will hear you, so think as positively about yourself as you want.

Lest you be concerned that talking about yourself in a positive way will look like bragging, here are some guidelines: Reinforce the other person for achievements that you sincerely admire and show an interest in the other person — ask questions and comment on the things he/she says. Whatever you do, be sincere.

Also, "bragging" need not be competitive. *"I'm really proud of my abilities* as a chickenplucker" is much better than, *"Yessir! I'm the best* chickenplucker in 20 miles."

When it is your goal to able to *think* and *talk* about yourself in a positive way, it is a good idea to count both behaviors. Counting the number of times you *think* something is a bit tricky. What you can do is set a goal for yourself — how many times a day do you want to think something nice about yourself? With this goal in mind, you very purposely think nice thoughts about yourself. Don't sit around hoping you will accidentally think something good. If you are unable to think of anything positive about yourself, take a day or two to compile a list. Keep adding to the list as you go along. This list is a handy reference for those days you're down.

Let's say you set a goal to say something positive to yourself ten times a day. When you achieve that goal with ease, increase it to 14 or 15. It is necessary to "overshoot" your ultimate goal because there is a tendency to backslide a little when counting is discontinued.

The opposite of self-appreciation is self-depreciation. "The 'best' is good enough for others but too good for me" is not an uncommon attitude. One day a friend of mine was in the liquor store and a women customer was asking the clerk to recommend a brand of liqueur. The clerk suggested BOLS liqueur. She replied, "Oh, I don't need anything *that* good." The clerk explained that BOLS is a very fine liqueur and quite reasonably priced.

She protested, "You don't understand - I'm only getting it for myself." Our friend broke in, "Perhaps you would be interested to know that BOLS spelled backward is 'SLOB'." She bought the liqueur.

You have had years of practice in self-depreciation. It will take you a while to reverse the habit. Thinking positive thoughts about yourself is something you should keep right on doing — forever.

1. Reinforce yourself (to yourself) for something you say or do.
2. Say something positive about yourself during a conversation with one or two people you do not know very well.
3. Reinforce yourself for an assertive behavior.
4. Think of three things you like about yourself.
5. Reinforce yourself for improvement you have made.
6. Write a letter to friend or relative in which you state something positive about yourself.
7. Call someone. During the converstion, say something positive about yourself.
8. During a face-to-face conversation with people you know well, say something positive about yourself.
9. Tell someone about a situation you handled successfully.
10. Set a goal to think a given number of positive self-statements per day.

2. Feel Comfortable Expressing Honest Compliments

Most of us appreciate things about people — something they do, what they wear, the way they look, what they say, and so forth. Much of the time you may only appreciate people in your thoughts and not tell them what you like. I am suggesting that you tell them.

It is easy to forget to appreciate someone for doing things that "should" be done. You may think people should be responsible and dependable. But not everyone is. When they are, let them know you appreciate it.

Cooking is something that "should" be done, but the best cooks are those who get rave reviews for their culinary efforts. In our household everyone cooks, so we all know how much work goes into preparing a meal. It's great to cook for a verbally appreciative audience, so cooks are not hard to find in our household. And with all that reinforcement creativity abounds!

When your kid carries out the garbage, say "thank you." Better to give attention for doing it than for not doing it! Take the time to thank someone for doing an assigned task — after all, it is pleasant not to have to remind someone to do his share. Your environment is certainly much better when there is reinforcement going on instead of complaining.

Look at it this way: when you reinforce someone for doing what he "should" do, you are reinforcing that person for being responsible. The more responsible that person is, the less you have to worry about. On the other hand, the more you put yourself in a position of continually reminding everyone what their jobs are, the more you will have to worry about. Reminding people to do their work will become your job. You'll always be directing traffic — and that's a job.

An easy way to start off with giving reinforcement is to give non-verbal reinforcement. That is, you express yourself without words. You smile, nod your head, scrunch up your nose, pat, hug, kiss or wink. When you are comfortable with that, swing into verbal reinforcement. You can say things like "Thanks a bunch," "That's neat," "Wow," "I liked that," "I'm glad you did that," and "You did a good job." (I wanted to give you some hints about these matters, so you wouldn't have the excuse of not knowing what to say or do. You certainly aren't stuck with my ideas, though, so carry on.)

If you have already established a pattern of criticizing people for not doing things, you are probably quite good at spotting things you *don't* like. Good, at least you're observant! So just keep right on observing — only look for things you like. Now this won't be easy, because you'll have to give up nag, nag, nag. But you can do it!

A mother might think her job is a "thankless" one because no one ever tells her she's doing a great job. Because she never gets thanked, she thinks there is no reason for her to thank others. She could turn her "thankless job" into one that is more gratifying by "modeling" the behavior she wants. She can *demonstrate* the behavior by saying "thank-you."

I have a three-year old friend, Colleen, who is a very reinforcing person. Colleen thanks people for doing things for her — why, she even thanks her mother! When someone is wearing something she likes, she tells them. More than that, she is aware of the beauty of her environment. You may not be surprised to know that Colleen's mother is a very reinforcing person. Colleen is young enough to learn assertion from scratch. For you it may be necessary to *start over*.

To get a clear picture of what's happening with your behavior, break it down. Count the number of times you reinforce people in general *and* count the number of times you reinforce people you live with. You'll be able to see whether you are nicer to people away from home than you are with the people at home.

The more reinforcing *you* are, the more reinforcement you will get. You know the old cycle, "She never thanks me, why should I thank her?" Well, you can break ye olde cycle by starting to reinforce.

My son, Craig, once complained to us that we *never* reinforced him. We thought we were reinforcing, but that if he didn't think so, we would improve. (We thought it was neat that he asked for reinforcement instead of feeling bad because he didn't get it.) We asked him to count the number times we reinforced him and the number of times he reinforced us. Craig discovered that he was getting about four times as much reinforcement as he was giving. As we continued with the program, though, he started reinforcing us more (and we all lived happily ever after.)

Small Beginnings

1. Smile at someone you do not know.
2. Give eye contact and a smile to someone you care for.
3. Thank someone for saying or doing something you appreciate.
4. Compliment someone for a specific behavior (e.g., "I like the way you express yourself.")
5. Touch someone and smile.
6. Touch someone, smile, then compliment them for something they said or did.
7. Tell someone you appreciate their love, friendship, help, support, or whatever.
8. Thank someone for doing something they "were supposed to do."
9. Thank someone for thanking you.
10. Set a goal to give a certain number of compliments each day.

Accept Compliments Without Embarrassment

Most of us have learned this weird behavior of acting like we don't appreciate compliments. We say, "What?! You like this old thing? It's so old and worn out, I can't believe you really like it!" My goodness, with an act like that, it is a wonder anyone risks complimenting us.

One time Bill told me he enjoyed the meal I had cooked, and that I was a good cook. I said, "Oh, it's nothing really. Just

13

ordinary food. I don't know how to cook gourmet dishes. I'm just a plain, ordinary cook." And he replied, "Okay, so you're not a good cook." That was the first time anyone took a compliment back, and I didn't like it. I kept thinking about it, and later that evening, I asked him to tell me I was a good cook. He reminded me that he had already tried to do that, and it didn't work out. "Tell me again," I asked. So he did. And I said, "Thank you." That time I got to keep the compliment.

If you like being reinforced, be gracious and say, "Thank you." You might even try giving eye contact and a smile! You'll certainly improve your chances of getting reinforced again.

Sometimes you won't agree with the compliment. "Gee, you look nice today," is a hard compliment to accept when your hair needs to be shampooed and your eyes are red. But to that other person those things may truly not be noticeable. Although you may not agree with the other person's perception of you the behavior of complimenting can still be reinforced. You can sincerely say, "Thank you for the compliment."

My friend, Rita, once told me she did not receive praise from her friends and family. Rita is a very accomplished woman. She has many talents and skills I admire. I knew I was one friend who praised her and yet she was not aware of it. During the remainder of the evening, I complimented her several times. Each time she passed right over it. She changed the topic of conversation or in other ways did not acknowledge what I had said.

Later, I asked Rita if she was aware of having been praised. She wasn't. I presented her with the facts. I had praised her six times!

She began counting the number of times she accepted compliments. She was amazed to find she *was* receiving an adequate amount of praise. She opened up a whole new world by making herself aware of others' appreciation for her.

At this point someone invariably says, "Yeah, but should I say 'thank you' when they're only trying to butter you up?" It certainly does no harm to be courteous in the face of such fierce treachery! If your mind reading was inaccurate, then at least you have not been rude.

Many of the ten assertive behaviors will bring about changes others admire. Accept their compliments by saying, "Thank you," "I'm glad you noticed," "It was nice of you to tell me," "Thanks for the feedback," and so forth.

You may want to record your number of opportunities to accept compliments (in other words, the number of times you were complimented.) Keep track of how often you accepted the compliment versus how often you did not accept the compliment. Set a goal to improve this figure.

4. Express Yourself Directly and Spontaneously

Most people are so afraid of going out on a limb that they stay treed for most of their lives. Telling others what you think or how you feel does involve a bit of a risk — a risk many people never venture to take.

Since most relationships are founded on the feelings of one for the other, it seems reasonable that feelings should be expressed honestly. Often, though, people more aptly voice the feelings they "should" have rather than stating the feelings they actually do have. The feelings expressed, then, are not honest — they are only mirrors of expectations.

A grandmother may tell her friends that she just loves having her grandchildren visit without their parents, when she actually dislikes the responsibility. A husband may tell his wife his feelings are not hurt, all the while feeling as though he wants to cry.

Hiding feelings is easy. You can lie about them, pretend they don't exist, and you can even act one way and feel another. If you are successful at this, don't complain that nobody cares about your feelings.

Stating honest opinions does not mean that you must tell everybody everything on your mind. If a co-worker comes to work with a hangover, you needn't tell him he looks like "ten miles of bad road" — even if he does. If your date is wearing a horribly mismatched outfit, you needn't tell her she looks as though she got "dressed in the dark". There are simply times it is not important to give your opinion.

Now, if you decide not to comment and then the person asks for your opinion, you can give it. In such cases, it is wise to be tactful. You needn't *blurt* out all the awful truths of the matter.

Oddly, it's often easier for people to voice feelings of dissatisfaction than to verbalize feelings of caring. It may be easy enough for a father to call his teenage son a lazy, no-good bum, but extremely difficult to say that he loves him.

EXPRESS THE POSITIVE. When it comes to expressing yourself directly and spontaneously, start off with the positive. Statements of joy, pleasure, caring and love are likely to be well received by others. So, *say* those nice things you've only been thinking.

Positive feelings, in general, often go unsaid. If you've gotten out of the habit, others may think it seems out of character for you to exclaim how beautiful the clouds are today. Don't worry about what they think. If you want to comment on the beauty around you, then do it! Look about you and notice the pleasant sights and events.

When another driver lets you into his lane on the freeway, appreciate it. Let the driver know you appreciate his courtesy by flashing him a smile. When a store clerk is friendly and helpful, enjoy it. Tell the clerk you appreciate his friendly attitude. When your tomato bushes produce, be happy. Show the plants to friends and say how pleased you are with your gardening efforts.

Even when things go wrong, something is going right. Look for it. If you were to set a goal to become more aware of what's good about your environment, you could achieve that goal by simply counting the number of nice things you notice. When you accomplish that goal, you can set a new goal to verbalize your appreciation for the things you like.

People can't read your mind. They may think they know how you feel about them, but never feel quite certain. Reassure them you care.

Peggy and Harold had this mind reading problem. After twenty years of marriage, both had learned to take the other for granted. When Peggy complained to Harold that he never said, "I love you," he was startled. He thought that living with her was proof enough that he loved her.

People live together for a variety of reasons; love is not always one of them. If you live with someone *and* you love them, tell them you do.

Speaking of love, I wonder how many budding romances

don't get off the ground because the people involved are too shy to share their feelings. I have talked to men and women who are reluctant to say "I love you" to the person with whom they have a new relationship. This reluctance is generally due to the fear they will scare off the other person. This is a possibility. But it's also a possibility the relationship will come to an unnecessary end because neither party is aware of the other's feelings.

Anyway, isn't it best to begin a relationship on honest terms? If the relationship succeeds, you'll want the freedom to "be yourself," the freedom to say what you think and feel. So start off by being "yourself."

TOUCH ON THE "TOUCHY." You could say, "I don't like waiting for you. I would appreciate it if you would be on time for our next date." It's unnecessary to bring up that you have waited a total of 16 times in the past in snow, sleet, and hail. You needn't tell the person what an inconsiderate oaf he is to keep you waiting. You have expressed your dissatisfaction and your desire for his being on time. That's enough.

Sometimes people handle the most insignificant events like tragedies. For instance, many of us have gone through a meal with mayonnaise on our chin simply because no one had the "guts" to tell us about it. The more casually you handle it the more comfortable the other party will feel. Better to say, "Herb, you got mayonnaise on your chin," than to say "Herb, there's something I have to tell you. I don't know exactly how to tell you this, Herb. Herb, I want to be honest with you, Herb. That's why I've decided to tell you this, Herb. It's not that you're not a nice guy, Herb, and you shouldn't feel embarrassed in the least, but, Herb you've got mayonnaise on your chin."

Most people have learned to be crisis-oriented. They wait until a problem becomes really big and complicated before they attempt to deal with it. Instead of responding to the problem at the time it begins, they wait until they have stewed and simmered over it for weeks. By that time, what was once a small problem has taken on the aspects of a crisis.

This is particularly true of anger. It's as though expressing a little anger is embarrasing, but expressing a lot of anger is justified. Too many of us forget to deal with anger as soon as we feel it.

In order to avoid the negative results of expressing anger,

people often opt to "hold it in" — refrain from voicing anger. The anger that's being held in — where is it? That anger is your thoughts and the thoughts are stored in your memory bank. If we were to dissect your memory bank and let "it" all out, we would probably find this:

> He doesn't care about my feelings. It's useless to even try to get him to listen to me. All that would do is start a fight. Anyway if he did hear what I said, he would think it was dumb to feel like I do. He is so concerned about himself and what he wants he doesn't even have the time to be interested in what happens to me. He *says* he loves me, but he sure doesn't act like it. He probably doesn't love me anymore but is afraid to tell me. I don't know what I did wrong to make him quit loving me. I'm probably too emotional; I shouldn't let these things bother me. But they do. *They do!!*

These are all the thoughts that would go unsaid — until there comes the straw that breaks the camel's back. You blow up and out comes all those thoughts and accusations. You cry, holler and pout, but your relationship does not change. What's the matter? You vented your feelings, but you still feel awful. The problem is that nothing was resolved in all the heat. It would be much less harrowing to calmly express those thoughts as they occur, rather than bundling them all up and throwing them onto the fire at once.

Small Beginnings

1. State a positive opinion to someone you do not know well.
2. State a positive feeling to someone you do not know well.
3. During a discussion, say something in response to another's comment.
4. Say something positive about someone who is not present
5. Express a negative opinion to someone who is not close to you.
6. State a positive opinion to someone who is close to you.
7. State a positive feeling to someone who is close to you.
8. State a negative opinion to someone who is close to you.
9. State a negative feeling to someone who is close to you.
10. Set a goal to express your opinions or feelings a certain number of times a day.

5. Ask for What You Want.

A good place to start is to identify what you want. Many people know exactly what they don't want, but would be hard pressed to tell you what they do want.

He says, "I don't want to go there. We always go to the place *you* want to go to." She says, "Where would you like to go?" He says, "Oh, I don't know, where do you want to go?"

If you want to have some say in making plans, start off by making a suggestion about what you would like. The other person has a right to either accept or reject the suggestion. Should they accept your suggestion, you have not *forced* them to act against their will. Remember, they also had the right to reject the idea.

Ah! Fear of rejection. What if you ask for something and you get turned down? What if the other person rejects your idea? The end of the world, no doubt.

It is the fear of rejection that turns people into devious, underhanded, through-the-backdoor operators. You see, if you never come right out and ask for what you want, no one can come right out and turn you down. Of course, you really never know if they knew what you wanted, and you never know if you really got turned down. It is all pretty vague.

There are a lot of problems associated with being vague about your desires. For one thing you never know whether the other person received your messy message.

I used to be unhappy every time I got a letter from my mother. She did not respond to the things about which I had written. I wanted her to compliment me on my accomplishments, but she ignored them. One day I wrote and asked explicitly that she respond to things I wrote about and that she compliment me for things I had done. A funny thing happened. She did it.

She said she didn't know she hadn't been complimentary. After all, she had told all her neighbors about my accomplishments. Once she knew what I wanted, she gave it willingly.

Not all requests are granted. A request made of another person stands a chance of acceptance or rejection. Many people think they have "failed at assertiveness" if their request is denied. However, assertiveness is determined by your own behavior. The outcome of the request is irrelevant to ascertaining your assertiveness. You do not control the other person's behavior.

If you ask for a raise, you are assertive whether or not you get the raise. The supervisor then exercises his own judgment and rights in granting or refusing the raise. Learn to view your success in terms of what *you* do. Asking for what you want is the target behavior. Getting what you want is a bonus.

When you are direct about what you want, the other person doesn't have to try to interpret what you mean. Hinting about what you want is just a way of getting the person to jump through hoops — demonstrating they know how to do the trick of interpreting.

You are responsible for stating your desires in a straightforward way. Your chances of getting your desires met are certainly improved if the other person knows what you want.

"Gee, it sure has been a long time since we went out to dinner on Friday night," is hinting. "I would like to go out to dinner with you on Friday night. Sound okay to you?" is asking for what you want in very understandable terms.

"Would you please help me clean the basement?" is a request for help. Going to the basement alone, making noise, and grumbling a lot is a hint (a particularly annoying one!).

By the way, when you ask for help, don't expect to get it on a moment's notice. For those time-consuming tasks, speak to your potential helper a few days in advance to avoid conflict of plans. This allows everyone the freedom to make plans and not be accused of being uncooperative.

Often, you are faced with a recurring problem. The problem may be that your boss gives you assignments in plenty of time for you to complete them, *but*, from the assignment date to the completion date he constantly asks you if you are finished yet. You would rather he said, "How are you doing," instead of, "Are you about finished with the assignment?" Pick a time to discuss this with him other than when you are actually dealing with the problem. For instance, if he usually mentions it to you in the afternoon, make a point to see him before lunch to ask for what you want. You could say,"John, I would like to talk to you about the assignments you give me." Give him an opportunity to respond to what you say. Then tell him, "I would like for you to ask me how I'm doing rather than ask me whether I'm almost finished. It's a small issue, I know, but it's important to me. I'd appreciate it if you would do that for me."

It is up to you to determine what is appropriate to ask for and of whom you can ask it. Some relationships do not allow for an open exchange. In some cases this is a reality; in others it is a copout. You will have to take a close look at your own situation and see which it is for you.

One way to make this determination is to see, for instance, how your boss interacts with other employees. Do you see other employees successfully responding to your boss the way you would like to? Are you the only employee your boss seems to take advantage of? If others are successful in speaking up to the boss, then we have to say you too can be successful. If you are the only one he takes advantage of, it could be due to your lack of assertion.

As a general rule, in difficult situations you can ask yourself two questions: 1) What have I got to lose by asking or not asking? and 2) What have I got to gain by asking or not asking? This helps you weigh the risks involved.

Keep in mind the two questions are only a general rule. It's not a slick technique you can apply to every single situation.

Practice asking for what you want in low risk relationships first. Deal with high risk relationships only after you've experienced success elsewhere.

Small Beginnings

With someone you do not know very well:
1. Ask for an opinion.
2. Ask for a clarification or elaboration of what they have said.
3. Ask for reinforcement for something you are proud of.
4. Ask for a favor.
5. Ask for a behavior change (e.g., "Could you please speak more loudly?")

With someone you are close to:
1. Ask for an opinion.
2. Suggest an activity that you could do together.
3. Ask for reinforcement for something you are proud of.
4. Ask for a favor.
5. Ask for a behavior change (e.g. "Would you please ask me out a little more in advance?")

6. State Honest Disagreements with Ease

When you disagree with what someone says, stick to the issue. Most problems arise when one forgets to argue the issue and starts attacking the other person.

Disagreements need not lead to quarrels and fights. They often do, though, and that is why most people avoid disagreements like the plague. You can avoid a potentially ugly scene if you refuse to engage in dirty warfare.

First, try your hand at disagreeing with small, unimportant matters in low risk relationships. You'll get a feel for simply stating a disagreement and also for the strategies people use to get you off the track.

An example of a low risk relationship: you are riding the bus and you are seated next to someone you have never seen before (and probably won't see again). An example of a small unimportant matter: you think the bus service is satisfactory; he thinks it is poor. He says, "They should give free bus rides in the city. The service is inadequate. We shouldn't have to pay one cent for it." You say, "I don't know exactly what you have experienced in the way of poor service. My experience with the bus system here compares favorably to other systems I've used. The buses run frequently and they are on time. Sometimes the bus driver is even friendly — I consider that a bonus!" He says "Well, you must not use the bus much, or you'd know the service couldn't be worse." You say, "I use the bus twice a day. Maybe I've been lucky." As you get off, he's still grumbling about "poor service."

When you disagreed, you did not criticize him for his attitude. You stated your opinion *and* the specific reasons for forming your own opinion. You did not attempt to reform him. You asserted your point of view.

When you are able to speak on unimportant issues, begin asserting yourself in low risk relationships on issues of greater importance. For instance, the person on the bus sees you reading a book on assertiveness and states that it's all a bunch of hooey. You disagree, assertively.

Then move into slightly more involved relationships. Someone you occasionally see at parties would fit into this category. When you can successfully disagree on subjects such as music, sports heroes, good brands of liquor, or tennis teachers, move on to more involved matters. This year's political candidates, your taste in friends, traditional sex roles, or personal causes are subjects you are likely to be more vehement about. If you can carry on a disagreement at this level and keep collected, you are ready to deal with high risk relationships.

Disagree on small issues first. Only when you can successfully handle small issues do you get more into the complex areas. Take one step at a time. Get your footing, then move up.

Some disagreements will lead to arguments. When that happens, try to settle the argument instead of attempting to "win it." Whenever there's a winner, there's a loser — probably a sore loser at that. When an argument is resolved, all participants are winners.

When your goal is to resolve the problem, your behavior looks (and sounds) quite different from when you are trying to "win." The verbal jabs, name-calling, digging up the past and other deliberate attempts to hurt the other person have no place in an argument in which the goal is to reach a resolution.

You can learn to concede a point — how to say "I was wrong." If the other person's evidence is more reasonable than yours, say so. Don't remain committed to a point you can no longer justifiably sustain.

An apology may be in order at some point. If you have made an accusation which proves untrue, apologize for your error. If you get angry about something which is later clarified, apologize for your mistake and thank the other person for straightening it out.

When you and another person who is close to you hold opposing points of view, you may agree to disagree. If you perceive it as a "mountain" and he perceives it as a "molehill," let it be. No two people are going to have matching perspectives on all subjects. Accept that. When it appears the argument can be ended, bring it to an end.

Small Beginnings
1. Play the devil's advocate in a small group discussion.
2. When someone states an opinion you disagree with only slightly, say so.
3. When someone places a different interpretation on a "fact" from yours, state your opinion.
4. When someone cites a source of information, and that information differs from your source, cite your source

and state your difference.

5. When you have no opinion or belief about a subject discussed, pick a point of view that differs from that of the majority.
6. When someone tells you the reason why they think you said or did something and they are incorrect, tell them so.
7. When someone proposes a solution to a problem and you do not agree with that solution, give an alternative solution.
8. Ask a person you disagree with if they would mind reading a particular book or article that supports your point of view.
9. When you and another person vehemently disagree about something, propose a negotiation to resolve the difference.
10. When you and another person vehemently disagree about something, ask them what they think should be done to resolve the difference.
11. With someone you do not know very well: 1) disagree with what someone said in a newspaper or on television, 2) disagree with an incorrect statement of fact, and 3) disagree with an opinion.
12. Try each of the above in No. 11 with someone you are close to.

7. Be Able to Say "No"

If you are a person who feels others take advantage of you, you are a person who has not learned to say "no". *Others can not take advantage of you without your implicit permission.* The responsibility for saying "no" rests with you. It is not the other's responsibility to *not* ask the favor.

Saying "yes" when you want to say "no" is dishonest. It puts others at a disadvantage — they believe you made a choice to say "yes" because you meant "yes."

You deceive yourself if you think that your saying "yes" when you mean "no" avoids hurt feelings. The feelings you hurt are your own.

There are many 40- to 50-year-old women in my classes who come for the sole purpose of learning to say "no." These women are wives and mothers who are in the habit of doing for others first and putting themselves last. As the children of these women approach maturity, they begin to notice they have a martyr for a mother. Seeing that their mother cannot say "no", they stop asking. They do not want to "take advantage" of Mom because this leads to her pouting. Since she is unable to say "no," the only solution for the child is not to ask. The child may resent Mom for resenting him.

This cycle is basically dumb.

One mother, Marge, put her children before herself during the years the children lived at home. Marge thought she would have the next years to herself. Wrong. The kids had learned to depend on Mom. She was a great little seamstress. She was now sewing for her own kids *and* for her grandchildren. She did not mind sewing for the kids. What she did mind was her kids' expectations of her. They thought it was their right. They were not especially appreciative of her efforts. There was also a demand of time. Material received on Friday was expected in the form of a completed garment on Monday.

Marge learned to say "no" to both quantity and time expectations. She also asked the kids to thank her. She even went so far as to ask for tradeoffs. "I'll sew if you'll help me in the garden on Tuesday." What she ended up with was honest reciprocity. No longer all give, but a give and take.

Another student, Sheri, pointed out that in certain circumstances we have been taught that "no" means "yes." Sheri found that when she said "no" to sexual overtures, the man proceeded as though she had said "yes." This happened several times and each time she thought the man was extremely inconsiderate. One night it occurred to her it was possible the guy didn't understand what *she* meant by "no." She said to her date, "Look, when I say 'no', I always mean 'no.' When I say 'yes,' I always mean 'yes.' And I never say 'no' when I mean 'yes.'" This act of defining her terms saved Sheri from the hassle she had previously encountered.

Saying "no" is apt to meet with resistance on occasion. The individual who receives your "no" for an answer may feel rejected, angry or resentful. Or, he may be inconvenienced. In any of these events, there will be attempts made to get you to say "yes."

A friend to whom you have often loaned your car asks to borrow your car. You reply, "I'm sorry, but I can't loan you the car today, it's not drivable." Friend: "I really need it. This is my last opportunity to interview for this job. The only way I can get there is if I use your car." You: "My car is not drivable. The brakes are all gone." Friend: "That's okay. I can manage. I'll be extremely cautious. I'll take responsibility if anything happens." You: "No, Sam, I won't let you drive my car in its present condition. I suggest you take a bus to the interview. I know it will take longer, but it's far safer."

Friend: "What kind of friend are you anyway? I've been out of work for six weeks and you don't care whether I get a job or not: This is a pretty dirty trick to play on me. You can't trust anybody to be a friend." You: "I'm your friend. I care. That's why I won't let you drive a car without brakes.'"

Your friend first tried to persuade you to change your mind. When that didn't work, he resorted to accusations. You attempted to explain to your friend the circumstances, and yet you were not overly apologetic. You held your ground and proposed an alternative. You acted in your friend's best interest, although he certainly didn't appreciate it.

More often, you will want to say "no" when it is in your *own* best interest. This will be a more difficult "no" to say.

Your friend calls and asks you to watch his child. It's Sunday, and you have plans to stay at home — alone. You reply, "I don't care to take care of Kelly today, John. Thanks for asking me, though." John: "What are you doing? Are you going someplace?" You: "I'm not going anywhere. I'm staying at home and taking care of me." John: "Well, since you're not doing anything important, couldn't you watch Kelly for an hour or so? Anyway, old buddy, I think you owe me one." You: "I'm sorry, John, but I won't babysit for Kelly today. Please ask me some other time though."

You staunchly, but politely, stuck to your decision to stay alone. Friend John steadfastly stuck to his objective — trying to get what he wanted from you. If you give in to John's persuasion, you make it increasingly difficult to say "no" in the future. John would soon learn that the more pressure he applies, the surer he is of getting what he wants. John may be temporarily angered and inconvenienced because you said "no." However, if you said "yes" you would be temporarily angered and inconvenienced. It was reasonable to opt for the solution that favored yourself.

There are times friends ask inconvenient favors. Since they are your friends, you may choose to do the favor no matter how inconvenient. If you want to do it, then do it. I'm not suggesting you do favors only if they are convenient. I am suggesting, though, that you do inconvenient favors only if you *want* to.

There will be times you say "no" but decide to say "yes" because new information sheds light on your decision. You needn't be the immovable object. But continue to make your decision based on information, not intimidation.

When you extend favors repeatedly the recipient soon begins to expect your services. It is clearly a case in which privileges extended soon become rights. A request for a favor has the anticipated outcome of your saying "yes."

It is best you let others know ahead of time that there will be a change from the norm. If you have given freely of your time, give notice you will no longer be doing so.

If you have let yourself be taken for granted, you will encounter some of the same difficulties mentioned above. You have always volunteered to serve on a certain committee. You have not been officially asked this year, but you will be. Call the director of the organization and let him know you will not be available this year. Recognize you have trained others to take you for granted. It will require effort on your part to ease yourself smoothly out of the picture.

Be tactful. "No, I won't do it for you," is a very strong "no." "No, I don't care to do it," says the same thing more tactfully. "No, I won't, and I wish you would quit asking me to do things for you all the time," may express what you are thinking, but it is rather harsh. "No, I don't care to, Karen. This is one thing I don't think I'll ever want to do. I would appreciate it if you wouldn't ask me again. I'd rather not deal with it and it would be easier for me if you didn't bring it up."

When you say "no," express your thoughts and feelings simply. Don't get into a long, drawn out explanation as to why you choose to say "no". For instance, if you are unable to accept an invitation, you can simply say, "No, I can't go with you tonight. I'm really glad you asked me, and I would like to take you up on another time. Shall we make plans now to get together later?"

Compare this to a long, drawn out explanation of, "Gee, I'm really sorry I can't go. But I've just had the worst day. First, I got up late this morning and so I got to work late. Things have been going awful all day. Every customer I talked to was cranky and the freeway was a fright tonight. I'm just a nervous wreck and would be terrible company. I'm sure you can get someone else to go with you. But, I'm sorry I can't go."

At first a "no" may be taken as a form of rejection. As soon as the other person learns, however, that you are simply being honest, rejection is not likely to be an issue. A "no" is not a rejection of the person, but a rejection of the request. Make it clear what you are saying "no" to.

Your friends and family may not only survive your saying "no" but may be pleased to see you taking an interest in yourself for a change.

Small Beginnings

Ask a friend to help you with this. Tell your friend you need practice in being able to say "no." Ask your friend to make several requests of you, many of which you will say "no" to. You can then ask your friend how you did. Get feedback as to whether you were tactful and direct or whether you were apologetic and wordy.

When you are in a situation where it really doesn't matter whether you say "yes" or "no" — say "no." Work toward feeling as comfortable saying "no" as you do when you say "yes."

Practice saying "no" by occasionally refusing something small — like a coke or a cup of coffee.

8. Insist on Fair Treatment

This involves you and a person in a position of authority. A person in a position of authority could be someone who tells you that you must have a receipt in order to return the shirt your grandmother sent you or it could be someone who tells you that you don't have the proper credentials for a loan.

When you are dealing with people in business relationships, explore your alternatives. The "authority" who meets the public is rarely the one in charge. If you think you have been treated unfairly, ask to speak to the "authority's" supervisor. If you still are not satisfied, call or write the president of the organization. If you are dissatisified with the policy of the business, do not "take it out" on the assistant to the assistant of the assistant vice president.

Voicing your dissatisfaction in polite, yet firm terms may serve your purpose. Mistreatment of the person waiting on you will lead nowhere. No one will go out of his way to help a customer who treats him abusively.

If you are denied a loan, insurance coverage, or a job, find out why. Perhaps there was a misunderstanding which can be cleared up. Or, perhaps your qualifications did not meet the set criteria. Find out what you can do in order to meet the criteria at a later date. Be persistent, yet polite.

Recognize the limitations of the system within which you function. At work, for instance, you do not have the same right to criticize your boss's work that he has to criticize yours. In secondary schools the student is expected to follow a set of rules that do not apply to teachers. You can insist upon fair treatment to the degree your system affords it.

If you are unhappy about the limitations placed upon you, direct your energies toward change. Your insistence upon fair treatment could mean you initiate a petition, attend meetings, write letters, or form a committee to appeal.

A feeling of helplessness may prevail when you have stood up for your rights but are denied what you believe to be fair. When you have done all you can, learn to live with the results. You will only add to your feelings of helplessness if you allow yourself to be upset about what you cannot change. Remember, the world is not the way it should be.

Whatever the outcome, you'll feel a whole lot better for having stood up for your rights.

Small Beginnings

You cannot arrange situations in which you will need to insist upon fair treatment. Some general guidelines would be for you to:

1. Ask questions about something you do not understand.
2. Ask for a denial of a service or credit to be reevaluated.
3. Check to see whether the person in the position of authority needs more information from you in order to give you proper consideration.
4. Find out from public agencies what your rights are if you think you have been denied that which is due.
5. Ask to see a person in a higher position if you are not treated cordially by the person who meets the public.
6. Write a letter to the person in charge when you are not satisfied with treatment you received.
7. Don't give up. As long as you are making some headway, pursue the trail.
8. Make your expectations.
9. Feel free to take your business elsewhere if you are dissatisfied with the service offered.

9. Keep in Touch with Friends

Inertia and irrational thinking are the two greatest enemies of friendship. Many friendships end because neither person acts to keep it going, or because either or both persons are sitting home believing the other does not care.

Inertia is apt to creep up on you at the worst possible times. During a depression, a chat with a friend would be most welcome. Yet due to your depression, you do not push yourself to arrange a get-together. In your depressed state you are probably thinking no one likes you; therefore there is no one to call. The worse you feel, the more you isolate yourself.

You can overcome your inertia by making a deal with yourself. The deal could be that you can't have your morning coffee until you call and invite a friend over. Or, it might be that after you write a letter to a friend, you can read a book, or do your shopping, or take a shower.

The idea is to require yourself to do something difficult (e.g., call or write a friend) before you allow yourself to do something enjoyable (e.g., have coffee, read, shop, shower). This will work only if you keep a deal with yourself.

If you tend to be passive about arranging dates with friends, it is possible you'll end up being alone on the nights you would like to have company. This inaction can lead to your feeling hurt, rejected, or depressed.

Waiting for others to take the initiative is a luxury you cannot afford because it does not always have the desired results. In the above case, it means you might end up being alone on a Saturday night when you prefer to be with a friend. You may sit at home, alone, *wishing* you were somewhere else. Make plans right then to call a friend and make a date for next Saturday.

An irrational thought is a thought which is counter-productive — a thought which keeps you from reaching your long-term goals.

The type of irrational thinking which interferes with the continuance of a friendship sounds like this: "He didn't call me; he doesn't care for me." "I *think* she saw me, yet she didn't speak. She ignored me because I probably did something that made her angry with me." "They refused my invitation to dinner because I'm a terrible hostess." In most cases, there is no evidence to support your thoughts. You say these things to yourself and then act as though they are true.

You won't call him if you *think* he doesn't care for you. You won't call her because you *think* they think you're terrible. All of your irrational thoughts prevented you from making further effort to continue the friendships.

A women student, Linda, was working on "Keep in Touch with Friends." She decided to call a woman friend to whom she had not talked in a long time. She called her friend's office — three times. Since her friend was out each time, she left a message for the friend to return her call. Linda was about ready to give up. She began thinking her friend was purposely avoiding her. She then realized that that may not be true and decided to make one more call. This time her friend was in, they made a date, and had a great time catching up on each other's lives. (None of the messages had gotten through!)

In Chapter 8, Mind Tricks, you will learn how to get rid of those irrational thoughts.

When you begin to think you are friendless, look at your own behaviors. See if there isn't something you can do to improve your situation with old friends.

Small Beginnings

1. Call a friend.
2. Write a friend.
3. Invite a friend to do something social with you.
4. Invite a friend to attend a class, workshop, or seminar with you.
5. Pick up a small gift for a friend and give it to her/him.
6. Tell a friend you would like to come for a visit and find out if that's okay.
7. Invite a friend to join you and another person in a social activity.
8. Throw a party.
9. Invite several friends to a buffet dinner.
10. Have a potluck dinner.

10. Take the First Step in Forming New Friendships

When you see someone you would like to know, do something about it. Instead of letting opportunities slip by, take the first step — the first risk.

Some enchanted evening, you will meet a stranger — then what? You'll wait to see what happens. Right? Wrong.

When you meet someone you would like to know better, act on that desire. If you wait for them to act, you assume that they are capable of assuming risks. Risks are risks no matter who takes them. Ask no more of others than you ask of

Passive behavior can easily be justified by your own thoughts. "She appears to have many friends already. She wouldn't be interested in knowing *me*." "No use introducing myself, I have nothing interesting to talk about." "I know he wouldn't like a woman who goes to him." Your thoughts are not *evidence*. You may *think* she doesn't need any more friends, *but* you do not *know* she doesn't. Let *her* decide that.

Practice taking the first step by smiling at the person standing in line next to you, by talking about the weather with someone you do not know, by asking for information from someone you have not met, or by asking a question.

One of the funniest opening lines I've heard took place on a city bus. It was a Friday. An old fellow got on the bus and said to no one in particular, "Boy, I hope I never have another day like last Tuesday." I was hooked; I asked him what happened last Tuesday.

I am not suggesting you use his line, but I am suggesting you find and use opportunities to talk to others.

Small Beginnings

1. Introduce yourself to someone who appears to be interesting.
2. Reintroduce yourself to someone you met briefly.
3. Ask this new person if he/she would like to get together with you for lunch.
4. Call this new person and invite them to go someplace with you.
5. Go to a party where there will be several people you don't know.
6. Accept an invitation to do something with someone you've just met.
7. Make a suggestion that you and several other newly-acquainted people do something together (such as go out for a beer after a meeting).
8. When you see someone you recently met, go up to them and start a conversation.
9. Ask this new person questions and get his/her opinion, such as, Did you see such-and-such movie? How did you like it? Have you ever been to this particular restaurant? How was the food?
10. During a class, a meeting, a party or other gathering, sit next to someone you don't know and strike up a conversation.

NOTE: When you want to get together with someone you don't know well, arrange to do so in a public setting. Most people feel more comfortable to be with someone they don't know during the daylight hours. It's better to play it safe in the beginning.

CHAPTER 4

SETTING AND ATTAINING GOALS

Problem Solving

When you have a problem, the basic question is whether you want to solve it. You will get more attention for complaining, but you still end up with a problem.

If you are seeking a remedy, consider these three alternatives:

1. You can change it.
2. You can avoid it.
3. You can tolerate it.

Suppose this is your problem: You hate your job. It doesn't pay enough and you have too much work to do.

You could attempt to change the problem by asking for a raise. Perhaps you would not think you have too much work to do if you were paid more. If getting a raise is not a feasible possibility, ask to have the workload reevaluated. Let your supervisor know that you think your workload is too heavy and you cannot do good work under those conditions.

If you are denied a raise and a change in work duties, you must decide whether to quit your job (avoid it) — or to stay there and put up with things the way they are (tolerate it).

If you decide the grass is greener elsewhere, then look for another job so you can quit this one. By working elsewhere you would *avoid* the problems of your current job.

If you decide that the grass is not greener elsewhere, you will have to elect to stay where you are. Since the other alternatives have been eliminated, then you must learn to tolerate the situation. Mostly this means you don't go around crying, "Poor me, I have to work at a job I don't like. The world is not fair. Why does this have to happen to me?" None of these statements help you tolerate the situation.

You tolerate the job by making statements to yourself like, "I have made my choice to stay, no use making myself miserable by going over and over what I don't like. I will look at the positive side of things. Complaining changes nothing."

You can use this same process for any type of problem, be it

33

with your children, parents, spouse, friend, colleague, boss, or a person in a position of authority.

When people talk about their problems, they don't have to be concerned with being successful in solving them. After an intense talk with a friend, chances are they will continue feeling and behaving the same as always.

I have high expectations that you will be able to make the changes you desire when you use the techniques I describe. So get ready, because things will soon begin to happen!

Know What You Want

You are probably quite aware of what you do not like about yourself. But do you know what you want to do to improve? What you want to be? I'll bet you don't.

So one of the first problems will be to figure out what you want. Not only that, but you will have to specify what you need to do in order to achieve what you want.

Perhaps you want to become a nicer person. Okay, now you know what you want. Next, you have to specify what behaviors will make you become a nicer person.

What do "nice" people do? They smile a lot, they give eye contact during conversation, they compliment others, they speak positively about people who are not present, they initiate greetings and they ask questions during conversations. We now have a list of behaviors, some of which you may want to adopt in order to become a nicer person. You may have other ideas about what a "nice" person does; you can add those to the list.

Perhaps you want to get in touch with your feelings. Specify the behaviors which will help you attain that goal. For example, you could express your feelings to others, express to yourself how you truly feel (instead of scolding yourself for not feeling the way you *should* feel), and you could be sure to do the exercises in this book that are designed to help you work on the way you think and feel.

Once again, you know what you must do in order to achieve your goal. Each time you have gone from a vague description of what you want, to a specific behavior. This is called pinpointing.

To determine if something is pinpointed, ask, "Is it *measurable*?" For instance, "Establish better communication with my husband" is a fine ambition. But it's not pinpointed because it's not measurable. Better would be "Express my feelings to my husband," or "Touch more often at times other than just when we're having sex," or merely, "Spend more time talking." Each of these is measurable.

Pinpointing behaviors gets you away from vagueness. It tells you what, specifically, to work on.

Some of the following behaviors are pinpointed. That is, they are measurable. Please indicate which they are.

1. Be more supportive of my wife.
2. Provide better releases from my pent-up energies.
3. Ask questions when I don't understand.
4. Get more into personal growth.
5. When I like somebody, tell them so.
6. Spend more time with my son.
7. Be more loving to my family.
8. Take better care of myself.
9. Spend time with the neighbors.
10. Be assertive.

The correctly pinpointed items are 3, 5, 6, and 9. All the rest would have to be broken down more, in order to be pinpointed.

Counting and Recording

What do you do when you "work to improve" a behavior? Glad you asked. You count it. That's right, you count it. Yes, it does sound too simple. One reason to count a behavior is that it is an effective way to bring about change.

Before you can begin counting, you need a target behavior. Specify what you want to improve. Pinpoint.

You should start with a fairly easy, non-controversial behavior. Set yourself up for success. After you have succeeded with some easy behaviors, you can work up to the more difficult ones.

Complimenting more often would be a good place to start. The first week all you do is count the number of times you compliment. The second week, you set a numerical goal slightly higher above the count of the first week. The third week, the goal is higher than the second. Keep doing this until you are complimenting as often as you would like.

TARGET BEHAVIOR: COMPLIMENT

Week	No. of Times
1	10
2	14 (goal: 12)
3	18 (goal: 15)
4	25 (goal: 20)

Notice how the goal was increased only slightly each week? You are expecting yourself to make small improvements each week. When you take small steps toward achieving your goal, you will probably attain it. The failure is likely to come when you set impossible goals — such as going from complimenting 10 times a *week* to 10 times a *day*. That is an unreasonable expectation of yourself and you stand a good chance of failing by the second week. Don't do that to yourself.

Some target behaviors can only occur as the opportunities present themselves. For instance, you can only accept a compliment without embarrassment if you are given one. Or, you can only say "no" if you are asked to do something you don't want to do. In these cases, you should record "opportunities missed" (give yourself a minus, "-") vs. "opportunities taken" (give yourself a plus, "+"). Then set your goal in terms of percentage. For instance, "I shall accept compliments without embarrassment 75% of the time."

Counting behaviors is a way to reinforce yourself. It is immensely more effective to record the count *immediately* following the behavior than to hope you will remember to do it later. As you record the count, you give yourself credit for an accomplishment. It's like a pat on the back, only this pat is to you, from you.

Counting behaviors produces an understanding and awareness of the behavior you are working on. Counting also acts as a reminder throughout the day to work on your target behavior.

As you record your daily scores on a chart, you have a precise, visual record of your progress. Records are important, especially on those days you feel you're not making headway. You will have your records to give you feedback.

Here's how to proceed:

1. Pinpoint the behavior (e.g., complimenting others).

2. Count each behavior.
3. Chart daily totals.

I prefer golf counters for keeping track of behaviors. Golf counters are available in most sporting goods or discount stores. The price is usually around $4. Most of them look like a Dick Tracy wrist radio and are terrific conversation pieces! Strangers will approach you to find out what you are wearing on your wrist. One thing leads to another, and first thing you know you are telling them about counting behaviors. If you are working on forming new friendships, you might want to keep this in mind!

If you don't want to be conspicuous, use a 3" x 5" index card. Carry it in your hip pocket or shirt pocket. Simply whip it out each time you have a behavior to record. Or you can use a knitting counter from a dime store. Choose a method you know you will use — if you don't use it, it won't work.

Making a chart of the totals will be additionally helpful. If you are counting something that happens often throughout the day, graph the daily total. If you are counting something that may happen only a few times during the week, graph the weekly total.

Here are some examples of a card that you might use and a couple of charts, one for daily recording and one for weekly recording.

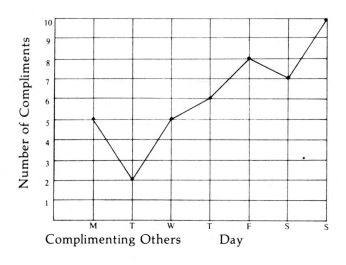

Complimenting Others   Day

37

	morning	afternoon	evening	
M	/	//	//	5
T	/	/		2
W	//	/	//	5
Th	//	//	//	6
F	/	THL	//	8
S	///	//	//	7
S	//	///	THL	10

Name: _Fritz_   Project: _Complimenting Others_   Total 43   Date 3/14

You can make a graph large enough to accommodate several weeks of data. This will show you how you are progressing from week to week.

There are many ways to do charting. I am showing you the easiest one. If you want to be more elaborate or creative, go to it. Make it fun to use.

Each plot (where the dot is) represents the total number for that week. During week one, the behavior occurred once.

Weekly Chart

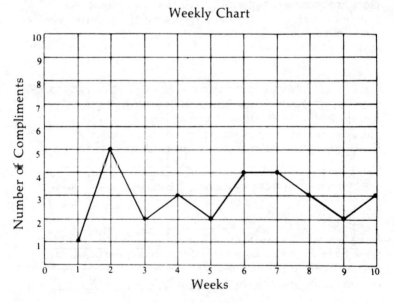

At our house we are always counting and charting something, and we post our charts on the refrigerator or in

the bathroom. Two reasons for this: we can reinforce
ourselves for improvements and we can reinforce each other.
If others in your household are interested in your goal, put
your chart where they can see it. Then they will be able to
reinforce you for your success.

You should make it clear to your family and friends that you
want only reinforcement from them. If you are not doing
well, your chart will give you all the feedback you need. You
don't need additional punishment in the form of snide
remarks and nagging.

Do Not Amputate Your Behaviors

Always work on improving a behavior. Do not work on
eliminating a behavior. When you successfully eliminate a
behavior, you do not automatically replace it with a behavior
you want.

If you are a person who complains a lot and you work to
eliminate complaining, you do not suddenly become a warm,
complimentary person just because you no longer complain.
If, indeed, you do complain a lot, when that behavior is taken
away, you will probably become a bump on a log. If you learn
no new behavior to replace the old unwanted one you are
left with nothing to say.

There was a woman, Nora, who wanted to eliminate being
anxious when she talked during class discussion. Until she re-
directed her goal, she eliminated anxiety by not talking. No
talking, no anxiety. What she actually wanted was to be able
to speak without anxiety, so she was far from achieving what
she wanted. We changed her goal. Before class began, she
specified how many times she would speak up during
discussion. The more opportunity she gave herself to speak,
the less anxious she was about speaking.

The goal to eliminate an unwanted emotion did not help her
achieve her goal, but pinpointing a behavior she wanted to
increase did help. The same is true for you. This helps to
identify what you want.

It may be scary to think about eliminating a behavior. You
think of it as giving up a part of yourself. You begin to
wonder what it will feel like to be missing a part of yourself.
It feels uncomfortable to give up a behavior.

When you develop a new behavior, you edge out the old
behavior. When you force yourself to speak up, you edge out

anxiety and gradually replace it with confidence. When you initiate conversations, you replace shyness with friendliness. This all feels quite nice. Not at all scary.

What If You Are Not Making Progress

Of course, there are times your records will indicate you are not making progress. This is important feedback too. If this happens, re-evaluate your goal. Perhaps you set a goal too high. If that is so, reduce it. Maybe you need to try an easier behavior.

You may have to follow the behavior with a reinforcer in addition to counting it. *When* you do the behavior, *then* what do you get?

My son, Craig, had very poor study habits. So he set himself up on a "when, then" program. When he was up at 7:00 a.m., then he would allow himself a hot breakfast. When he studied for 15 minutes, then he could read something for pleasure for 30 minutes.

All of the "thens" were things he enjoyed. All of the "whens" were things he wanted to do but was not usually motivated enough to do. The "thens" were his rewards for doing the more difficult behaviors. You might notice, he expected to study for only 15 minutes and could pleasure-read for 30 minutes. As it became easy for him to meet the 15 minute study goal, he increased it to 20 minutes and still allowed himself 30 minutes of pleasure reading. Soon he was studying for 30 minutes and pleasure reading for 30 minutes.

All of the "thens" in Craig's program that dealt with himself were events he was already doing. He simply arranged to *earn* them.

You may, for instance, decide that "when" you can give 15 compliments this week, "then" you will treat yourself to a long-distance telephone call to your friend in Tampa.

This is a beautiful way to discipline yourself. It works only when you take a contract with yourself seriously, though. If you allow yourself the "thens" without accomplishing the "whens," no purpose is served.

Using the Assertiveness Inventory

During the time you are working on one specific assertive behavior, you will want to keep in touch with the other nine assertive behaviors.

To help you keep focused on your general goal — to become more assertive — I am recommending you use the following "Assertiveness Inventory". The "Assertiveness Inventory" is your own daily assessment of how well you are doing overall.

Each evening sit down for about one minute and go over the inventory. Evaluate your behavior in each of the ten categories. Give yourself a letter grade for how well you think you did. If you did super well, give yourself an "A." If you did pretty well, rate that a "B". So-so would deserve a "C." Falling down on the job would get a "D". If you blew it entirely give yourself an "F".

Name _____ Week Beginning: _____

ASSERTIVENESS INVENTORY

At the end of each day, please give yourself a letter grade for each behavior.
If you did not have the opportunity to perform a behavior, write N/A (not applicable).

	M	T	W	T	F	S	S
Think and talk about yourself in a positive way							
Feel comfortable expressing compliments							
Accept compliments without embarrassment							
Express yourself directly and spontaneously							
Ask for what you want							
State honest disagreements with ease							
Be able to say "no"							
Insist on fair treatment							
Keep in touch with friends							
Take the first step in forming new friendships							

From Project You: A Manual of Rational Assertiveness Training by Claudine Paris and Bill Casey.
Copying this page is permitted.

CHAPTER 5
KEEPING MOTIVATED

Relationships and Change

Many relationships are based on one person's being generally passive, and the other's being generally aggressive. The more passive partner is hesitant to state an opinion or disagreement, while the more aggressive partner tends to make plans and give orders.

In either case, the person is using the behaviors that he/she has learned from experience to work the best. But, because the aggressor seems to have the upper hand, he/she is usually seen as having greater control over his/her behavior.

An example of this is when a husband (in this case, the aggressor) tells his wife he doesn't want her to work or go to school. He wants her to stay home and be a "good wife and mother." The wife may resent her husband's expectations of her but goes along with him rather than "making a fuss." Twenty or thirty years later the wife finds herself with no children in the house (and maybe no husband either) and blames her husband for "not letting" her go back to school or to have a career.

In fact, he was no more to blame than she (if, indeed, one finds it necessary to bother placing blame at all). He demanded something and she gave in. *Obviously, such relationships require two participants!*

If you are the aggressive partner and you are working on becoming more assertive, then your changes ought to go smoothly. As you begin to extend rights to your passive partner he/she may be a bit bewildered, but you are not likely to get punished for your efforts. Generally speaking, people who change their aggressive behaviors to assertive behaviors will find their environments supporting such change. However, if you are the passive partner and you are working on becoming more assertive, the going is a bit rougher. When the passive partner begins to state opinions and disagreements, the aggressive partner is apt to do some verbal punishing, e.g., "What do you mean you don't want to go?! I've decided we're going and that's it!" Or, "I suppose you think you are being assertive when you act like that. Well, you're not. You're being foolish." Or, "I don't need any bitching from you. Keep your stupid mouth shut. I'll handle it — just like I always have." Or, "Wrong, wrong. You simply do not know what you are talking about." "No one is interested in what you think. Just keep quiet."

There's also the sneaky-aggressive approach to punishment. Your partner refuses to speak to you. Or to have sex with you. Or to even touch you.

When all else fails, the guilt trip follows. "After all of the things I've done for you, this is the thanks I get." "Don't worry about me. As long as you're happy, never mind that I'm worried sick." Or, "You ruined the whole evening for the hostess when you refused to eat her dessert. It wouldn't hurt you to break your diet this once."

These people are using all the methods they know of to keep you in line. These ploys have worked before and it is expected they will still work - with just a little added pressure.

Try to respond to this verbal punishment in a calm, polite way. Don't get dragged into a quarrel by responding in kind.

The comment about the hostess and her dessert could be dealt with by your saying, "I was sorry the hostess felt hurt. However, I thought it was unnecessary for her to insist I eat. What I eat and when I eat will be a decision I make. I won't get fat just to make someone happy. I would like to have you reinforce me for standing up for what I thought was right."

In this reply you have not scolded your partner for his remarks. You have stated your reasons for making the decision. You have made clear your intent to continue to stand up for your rights. You have asked to be reinforced. Hopefully, you used a tone of voice that was polite, yet firm.

It is not uncommon for someone to label your attempts to be assertive as being aggressive. The remark would generally be, "You're not assertive; you're aggressive!" Since no specific incident was cited, you cannot agree or disagree. You might say, "I have been working hard to become more assertive. I do not intend to be aggressive. When I do something that seems aggressive to you, please let me know. That way I'll know exactly what you're talking about. If I agree that it's aggressive, I'll work to improve. I appreciate your letting me know what you think. I'd also like it if you would reinforce me when you think I'm being assertive."

You have tried to get more information and you have

indicated a willingness to change if necessary. You have reinforced the other person for being open with you. And, you have asked to be reinforced for assertive behavior.

When others scoff you will need to be your assertive best. Don't give in just because it is difficult. It gets easier all the time.

Allowing Labels to Hurt You

Labels have no magical power to turn you into whatever the label implies. *You* give labels power by believing them.

If someone calls you a "turnip" it doesn't *make* you a turnip. If someone calls you "stupid" it doesn't *make* you stupid.

One mistake does not make you "stupid" or "incompetent." Yet, if you give yourself that label or if someone calls you "stupid," you probably respond as though the label is accurate and meaningful.

Labels such as "stupid or "incompetent" have a great power because they are easily believed by the person being labeled. When you are called "stupid," you think, "He's right. I never do anything the way I'm supposed to." You subsequently feel awful, put down, or rejected.

Labels such as "brilliant" or "creative" lack power because the recipient of the label does not believe them.

When you figure out a solution to a problem and your supervisor tells you how brilliant you are — you probably don't believe it. You think "Anyone with an excuse for a brain could have figured it out." You then feel silly or embarrassed.

If someone calls you a turnip it is unlikely you will be upset or hurt. For most of us the label "pig" carries many meanings — it may mean you are dirty, lazy, fat or uncouth. In your head there may be yet other connotations for the label "pig." So, when someone calls you a pig, you read your meaning into the label and you feel hurt.

You have no doubt found yourself labeling your own behavior. It is often the labels, not the act itself, that you respond to. You assertively ask your friend out to dinner. Your friend changes other plans in order to accept. You then find yourself thinking, "I'm too *demanding* of his time. I shouldn't have asked him." You feel guilty.

I emphasized the word "demanding" because I want you to

notice how cleverly a label sneaked into your thoughts. Once you labeled yourself "demanding" you made the label convincing by backing it up with your next thought. Even though your friend accepted the invitation you are convinced (in your own head) that you are "demanding" — you asked for more than was right.

You go on to think, "I shouldn't be so *selfish*. He has other friends he likes to spend his time with."

Now, you have given yourself yet another label — "selfish." You feel awful, awful. Your thoughts get out of hand and you think, "I wish he had been *honest* with me. He didn't have to feel *pressured* into accepting."

This situation you created in your head is vastly unlike the situation which actually happens. You asked a friend to spend some time with you, he accepted. But, by this time, you have convinced yourself that you are demanding and selfish and your friend is dishonest. With all these unfounded, wild thoughts racing through your head, the chances of your having a good time with your friend look slim.

The process of negative labeling diverts you from the issue. These labels give you no real information (what does "selfish" mean?). They were counter-productive.

Of course, labels can have a positive effect. If you believe the words innovative, creative, efficient, talented, or honest, apply to you, then apply them. Be generous when applying positive labels to yourself — you'll like the way they make you feel.

Getting Support for Your Changes

You are ready now to start working on specific behavior changes. The changes you make will not only affect you, they will affect your relationships.

Let the people you live with know what your goals are — they will feel less threatened by your changes if they know what's going on. Tell them why you wish to make changes — why you want to grow. Ask them for their support and reinforcement. Assure them that the changes will make you happier with yourself, and will in turn benefit your relationship.

When others are having a hard time understanding your goals, be patient but firm with them. Explain again if necessary what you want to achieve and why. Don't be intimidated by their lack of understanding. They may have become accustomed to your old behaviors.

Making the decision to change is easy. Sticking to your decision is difficult. Whenever someone close to you criticizes your goals, you will waiver and wonder whether you are doing the right things. If you are sure you are doing the right thing, keep plugging away — their wariness will subside as you get better at what you're doing.

Furthermore, since even your supporters may neglect to reinforce, you will need to reinforce yourself. Besides, you are really the only one who can truly appreciate that you have done something difficult or remarkable.

Counting and recording have already been discussed as methods of self-reinforcement. Internal reinforcement is another. That is, you think to yourself, "I did it!" "That was well done." "I felt comfortable, not the least bit anxious." "Boy, that was impressive."

It is not uncommon to make statements to yourself about your behavior. Often, though, these self-statements are self-defeating. "Well, I finally did it. I probably looked real dumb." "I might as well give up now, it won't always work as well as it did this time." Don't quit talking to yourself, but please quit being negative.

If you think a lot of self-reinforcing thoughts, it is likely you will continue to improve the behavior you reinforced. Self-defeating statements interfere with progress. The more you put yourself down the less your chance of meeting your goals.

After You're Assertive, What Do You Think?

When you did something assertive, what did you think? How did it feel? What you think and how you feel about your own behaviors determines your continued success in assertiveness.

For instance, did you politely but firmly refuse to do a favor for a friend, then find yourself thinking, "I shouldn't have said 'no.' He didn't understand, even though he pretended to. He'll never do anything for me again. He's probably mad at me."

These are self-defeating thoughts and as such they produce feelings of guilt, remorse, anxiety or fear. I hope you recognize these thoughts for what they are — *punishers*. Such thoughts punish the very behavior you want to improve. Very bad!

If you want to be successful with assertiveness, you will have to work on thinking thoughts that commend the behavior. Thoughts such as, "Good! I stood up for myself! He seemed to understand and accept my answer. As long as I keep behaving in this way, people will know that when I do something for them it's because I really want to." These statements are self-enhancing thoughts, and will lead to your having good feelings about your assertive act. The better you feel about what you did, the more apt you are to do it again.

So, go ahead — be assertive. And ENJOY IT!

CHAPTER 6

GETTING YOUR HEAD READY

Beliefs

Our beliefs are constantly in a state of flux. As we mature, change our life style, or as we are influenced by others, we receive information which causes us to change.

Some people reach a certain state and from that time on make no changes. These people are generally referred to as rigid, inflexible, or stubborn, because no matter what new input they get, they never change their beliefs. That's their prerogative.

Others feel guilty about changing their beliefs for fear they are being disloyal to themselves or to the "way they were raised." These people often act in ways inconsistent with their beliefs but they pay their dues by feeling guilty. Guilt is a high price to pay for doing something you want to do. A better way would be for you to *determine for yourself* what you believe. This means you will need to question some of those old beliefs you automatically accepted in the past. What served a purpose in the past may not serve you well now.

I knew a woman, Maggie, who moved to Denver from New Jersey. Maggie wanted to live on her own in Denver. Her mother wanted her to live in New Jersey. Maggie believed that she ought to do what her mother wanted her to do, *but* her behavior of living in Denver was inconsistent with the belief. So she continued to live in Denver, but she felt guilty for going against her mother's wishes.

I suggested she challenge her old belief of "I must do what my mother says." After all, when a woman is 26 years old, it is quite possible she will lead a boring and uneventful life while trying to meet all of Mom's expectations!

Maggie changed her old belief to: "I have a right to do with my life what I choose." (This did not mean she would no longer concern herself with her mother's feelings.) Her visible behavior changed: she stopped feeling guilty.

Unless Maggie's mother was willing to change her belief of "Children should do what they are told," it is likely that her relationship with Maggie would be interrupted, or damaged. There is often a parting of the ways when two people operate under incompatible belief systems.

Some parents cannot communicate with their adult children because they do not see eye-to-eye. Rather than learning to accept each other's ways, they choose to be disapproving. They wait and hope for the relationship to get better; sometimes it does. It gets better when all or one of the parties "mellows"; that is, when someone changes their beliefs and expectations.

Responsibility for Your Behavior

You are responsible for your own behaviors. Accepting this responsibility is a prerequisite for change.

Most people admit responsibility for the way they act. However, your responsibility extends beyond behaviors that everyone can see. It extends to behaviors you can't see: your thoughts. Just because you're the only one who can detect their occurrence doesn't mean you can elude the responsibility. They are your thoughts, and you are in charge!

You may have never looked at thoughts this way. If not, you may be like a child who has never been held accountable for his actions. You seem to just do things without ever considering whether they are good for you, or could be changed. Thoughts *can* be changed. The following chapter will tell you specifically how to do this. First, however, you must accept that you can change them if you want to.

Emotions too are behaviors. And like thoughts, you are responsible for them. It is ironic how easily we accept the responsibility for other people's feelings, yet do not accept the responsibility for our own feelings.

The way we learn to express emotions actually puts the responsibility on the wrong person. *"He hurt my feelings." "She makes me angry." "My kids make me depressed."*

It's most accurate to make statements of emotion in the form of an "I" statement. "I feel upset about what happened." "I feel angry when you do that." "I feel depressed when I'm home with the kids all day." When you hear yourself make these "I" statements, you are hearing yourself accept the responsibility.

Until you are ready to accept the responsibility for your own emotions, you do not have the power to change the way you feel. You can conveniently blame others for your emotions, but the way you feel won't change until *you* act.

Your Internal World

The world you live in begins in your head. Your perception of events causes your world to be unlike mine — unlike anyone's.

The words, attitude, judgment, belief, perception, self-statement, and interpretation, are labels we give to the mental process "thinking." It is through this process you shape your world.

"Thinking" is a behavior. It is a behavior which cannot be directly observed by others, but it is a behavior. Kicking your foot or waving your arm are also behaviors. These behaviors differ from "thinking" in that they can be *seen* by yourself and others.

You see, hear, feel, taste, and smell stimuli from your environment. How you process ("think about") those stimuli determines how you respond* to them. The brain is constructed in such a way that you have to think before you can respond with either an action *or* an emotion.

It is the purpose of much of the rest of the book to help you think in such a way that you will be more assertive. There are some psychologists who contend that you must change your actions before you can change your thoughts. Others contend that you must change your thoughts before you can change your actions. The division is artificial. Since actions and thoughts are both behaviors, why not work on both at once?

Sometimes thoughts are hard to work on for the reason that **they seem automatic. Something happens and you "react** without thinking." This is because you have used some thoughts so much that they have become a part of a habit. These are "habitual thoughts." Some people call them "subconscious." I don't like to call them that because that makes them seem harder to get at than they really are.

Most habitual thoughts are beneficial. For instance, remember how hard you had to think about driving when you were first learning? It would be fairly annoying if these thoughts did not become habitual. And, as I sit here banging away at my old 1948 Underwood, I appreciate typing-related habitual thoughts. I am not aware of my brain saying "Now the 'A,' now the 'N'." Fortunately, it's all "automatic" (my thoughts, not the typewriter).

*With the exception of those few behaviors which are mediated at the spinal cord, such as pulling away from a hot stove.

I Think, Therefore I Feel

A lot of people believe that thoughts and emotions are the same thing. They are not. This confusion is evidenced when we hear such statements as, "I feel that she will be a great writer." Or, "I feel college would not be right for him." Clearly, these are statements of thought, not feeling.

This is not to say that the thought and feeling are unrelated. No indeed! As indicated earlier, thoughts cause feelings. Instead, the sequence goes like this: *situations* cause *thoughts,* which cause feelings. In that order.

From now on I'm going to ask you to be able to break down your experience into three parts: situation, thought, reaction. You will be spending quite a bit of effort cultivating this ability before you actually start working towards changing your thoughts. When you can change your thoughts, this will have a tremendous impact on your emotions. Although this three-part chain seems simple, it takes some practice to get it right. When you are done, you will be writing them like this:

Situation: Someone I don't care for asked me for a date.
Thought: "There's no way I can get out of this without looking like a rat!"
Reaction: Felt trapped, embarrassed; went on date.

Situation

The situation is the event that triggers the whole chain. The event may be external, such as "My wife thanked me for making the bed." The event may be internal, such as "I wondered if he still loved me." Or it may be both internal and external, such as "A person (external) I had long wanted to meet (internal) was standing in the elevator with me."

The only "don't" is this: Don't include your interpretation or value judgment of what goes on in your description of the situation. Judgments belong in the "thought" portion of the chain. *Try to keep the situation as objective as possible.*

Here are some correct samples:

—I received an invitation to a party.
—He called me stupid.
—I wanted to thank her.
—A woman I didn't know sent me a birthday card.
—She picked some of my flowers without asking.

Here are some examples which are incorrect because they include intepretations. The interpretations are in italics:

—He *tried to make me angry* with some *pretty sarcastic* remarks.
—She *buttered me up*, then asked me for a raise.
—She asked me to take care of her dog, *knowing full well that I owed her a favor.*
—I wanted to express happiness, but *they would probably disagree.*
—He gave me a *phony* smile.

Now let's see if you've got it. Out of the following ten situations, see if you can tell which are correct and which are incorrect:

1. He made some dumb attempts to make me feel guilty.
2. My mother asked for a ride—the fifth time that week.
3. He explained that I would have to wait in line.
4. She made some vicious comments about my dress.
5. They told stories which were probably supposed to be funny.
6. There's a fly in my soup.
7. She cried when I explained that I could not attend her daughter's wedding.
8. He tried to make me feel guilty.
9. I noticed that I was drooling.
10. She asked me why I was standing on her feet.

Numbers 2, 3, 6, 7, 9, and 10 are correct. Examples 1, 4, 5, and 8 are incorrect because they include interpretations.

Thought

Thoughts are triggered by the situations. This is the connection between your environment and your reaction to it. You cannot have emotion without first, on some level, thinking.

Here's another way to look at thoughts: they are your *beliefs* or *interpretations* about a situation. Take, for example, the situation "getting turned down for a date." Your belief may run something like, "This means that I am a clod, and no good!" Or, you may think, "Well, I'll just have to find someone nice who does want to date me." There are many different possible thoughts for any given situation. Some thoughts may be *rational* and some may be *irrational*.

When I mention "rational thoughts" or "irrational thoughts," I mean only this: Rational thoughts help you achieve your ultimate goals; irrational thoughts thwart you from your ultimate goals. I shall assume, since you are reading this manual, that assertiveness is among your goals. Therefore, counter-assertive thoughts like, "He doesn't want to meet me—I'm nothing," would be construed as irrational. On the other hand, pro-assertive thoughts like, "I'll introduce myself—I've got nothing to lose," would be construed as rational.

Often irrational thoughts help you with short-term goals Let's examine one of those thoughts: "It's too much trouble to tell the clerk that he short-changed me. It's only 75¢." This thought accomplishes the short-term goal of avoiding a situation that you feel uncomfortable with. On the other hand, it thwarts you from your long-term goal of insisting on fair treatment.

If you keep your long-term goals in mind it should be easy to tell which thoughts are rational and which are irrational. It's all a matter of getting where you're going. Thoughts that don't get you where you're going are irrational. See?

Naturally, it's rather difficult to determine the rationality of thoughts you can't specify. As discussed earlier, you will sometimes have a hard time identifying a thought. It will seem that you reacted automatically. In such cases, it is still possible to discover your thought. All you have to do is use a little deduction. Just ask yourself what, logically, you must have thought for that situation to produce that reaction.

Let's say you "automatically" got angry (reaction) when another driver honked at you for no apparent reason (situation). Surely you couldn't have been thinking, "He probably made an honest mistake—nothing to get angry about." Perhaps something a bit stronger? I'm sure you can think of a likely thought that would produce a little anger.

Now observe how the thought would differ if you "automatically" felt guilty in the same situation. Even though feeling guilty seems "automatic," the obvious thought must have been something like, "I must have done something wrong."

Here's the key: As long as you can specify the situation and specify your reaction, you can easily deduce your thought.

Lastly, you should be aware that all thoughts have a connotation or implication which you may or may not have expressed. For instance, the statement, "If I ask her for a date, she might turn me down," may well carry the implication that "that would be awful!" Or it could carry the implication "and that would be okay." The first implication would produce dread; the second implication would produce comparative comfort. Since it's accurate that she may turn you down, you must examine your implication to see if the thought is rational.

Here are some other examples where the thought is accurate, but the rationality depends on the implication. Look and see if you can think of at least two opposite implications for each one.

—The roads are not completely safe to travel on.
—If I called my old friend it's possible that he may not want to resume our friendship.
—Even if I say something positive about myself in the most courteous way it's possible that someone will think I'm conceited.
—My wife may not like it if I start sticking up for my rights.
—Learning to be assertive takes a lot of effort.

Sometimes you may have "mixed reactions" or what is mystically referred to as "inner conflicts." This is simply because you have several contradictory thoughts. For example, recall the times when you have given yourself a hundred reasons to do a chore, then put it off anyway. The procrastination, like any other reaction, is still the result of a thought. Even after all your internal lecturing, you still may have told yourself it would be okay to put off the chore another day.

Putting It All Together

Let's put it all together now. Situation, thought, reaction. Here is a series of examples:

Situation: I see someone I think I know.
Thought: "I'd like to say 'hi,' but I'd look foolish if he isn't the person I think he is."
Reaction: Feel shy — don't greet him.

Situation: My family doesn't notice all the work I've done around the house today.
Thought: "I should ask them to thank me."
Reaction: I ask them to thank me — feel okay.

Situation: I notice that my new suit was not altered correctly to fit me.
Thought: "Those dirty rats can't do anything right!"

54

Reaction: Angry — yell at tailor.

Situation: My husband compliments me on dinner.
Thought: "I'll look conceited if I act like I notice."
Reaction: Feel embarrassed — pretend I don't notice the compliment.

Situation: I would like to ask the boss to have lunch with me.
Thought: "He'll think I'm buttering him up."
Reaction: Regretful — don't ask him.

In each of the following examples there is at least one mistake. Try to discover what it is, then check with the answer at the end:

1. *Situation:* My mother tried to make me feel guilty.
   Thought: "She's up to her old tricks!"
   Reaction: Anger — walked out of the house.

2. *Situation:* My neighbor asked me to babysit for her.
   Thought: "She'll be impossible to be around if I say 'no.'"
   Reaction: I say "okay" because I'm afraid of what she will try if I don't.

3. *Situation:* I am standing at bus stop with someone who looks interesting to know.
   Thought: "It might be fun to get to know that person."
   Reaction: Feel shy and don't say anything anyway.

4. *Situation:* My son makes a statement that he knows I disagree with.
   Thought: "The best way to handle this is to disagree with what was said in a calm, matter of fact way."
   Reaction: Disagree — feel uncomfortable.

5. *Situation:* I decide that I would like a raise.
   Thought: "It doesn't hurt to ask."
   Reaction: Afraid — don't ask.

Here are the answers:

1. An interpretation was placed in the situation that my mother's motives were to make me feel guilty. Better would have been to simply cite the mother's behavior, such as "My mother told me about all the long nights she stayed up with me when I was a sickly child." The suspicions about her motive can go in the thought part.

2. The reaction includes a thought (because I'm afraid . . .). It

would be correct to say something like, "complied — felt resentful."

3. A common mistake. The reaction did not logically follow the thought. Even though at some point the individual may have had that thought, they must also have had (and should have written) a thought like, "He probably wouldn't be interested in me."

4. The situation part includes an interpretation of the son's behavior. This suspicion can go in the thought part. Better would have been: "My son says something I disagree with."

5. Same problem as Number 3. Again, the reaction did not logically follow the thought. The thought was probably, "I'd better not ask for a raise or the boss will think ill of me."

Now, I've got just one more exercise for you before we leave this section. Below is a list of ten assertive behaviors. Listed with each are two irrational thoughts which prevent assertion. Write three more for each assertive behavior.

THINK AND TALK ABOUT MYSELF IN A POSITIVE WAY

It is better to be humble.

I should give them a chance to compliment me first.

_____

_____

_____

FEEL COMFORTABLE EXPRESSING HONEST COMPLIMENTS

They won't accept it.

They never compliment me, so why should I compliment them?

_____

_____

_____

ACCEPT COMPLIMENTS WITHOUT EMBARRASSMENT

I don't want to look conceited.

They probably don't really mean it.

_____

_____

_____

EXPRESS YOURSELF DIRECTLY AND SPONTANEOUSLY

They might take offense.

It will seem aggressive.

_____

_____

_____

ASK FOR WHAT YOU WANT

I'll seem pushy or bossy.

I'm already too demanding.

_____

_____

_____

STATE HONEST DISAGREEMENTS WITH EASE

I know it will only start a fight.

My opinion isn't that important.

_____

_____

_____

BE ABLE TO SAY "NO"

They won't like me anymore.

They might get angry with me.

_____

_____

_____

INSIST ON FAIR TREATMENT

I don't want the hassle.

I don't deserve fair treatment.

_____

_____

_____

KEEP IN TOUCH WITH FRIENDS

It is their turn to contact me.

It is their responsibility.

_____

_____

_____

TAKE THE FIRST STEP IN FORMING NEW FRIENDSHIPS

I don't know what to say.

They don't want to meet me anyway.

_____

_____

_____

Arguing with Yourself

The way most people get rid of irrational thoughts is by arguing with them. This is when we fight irrational thoughts with reason. It's something most people do so naturally they don't even know they are doing it. In scary movies, for instance, we often tell ourselves, "It's only a movie." When a child acts rudely, we may remind ourselves that, "He just doesn't know any better." When a foreigner behaves in a way that we find strange, we may say to ourselves, "Of course he acts differently, he's from a different culture." All of these examples are intended to calm us down a little.

Here are a few examples of irrational thoughts and arguments:

Irrational thought: "I'd like to call my old friend, but if she hasn't called me by now, she probably doesn't want to talk to me."
Argument: "Ridiculous! If I want to talk to her, it's my responsibility to call her."

Irrational thought: "I probably shouldn't ask the gas station attendant to wash my windshield. He looks like he's got other things to do."
Argument: "That's just part of the job. And it's part of the 'service' I pay for at service stations."

Just follow one general rule when you are using these arguments with your irrational thoughts: *BE PERSUASIVE.* However, this rule has several implications.

First keep your arguments based in reality. When you don't, you will only be "rationalizing" — using arguments that are full of air. For instance:

Irrational thought: "It's catastrophic that my girlfriend got angry with me."
Ineffective argument: "I'm sure she's not mad, despite throwing all those dishes at me."

Irrational thought: "If I ask for vacation time now, my boss will probably think I'm a lazy good-for-nothing and will hate me."
Ineffective argument: "No, he won't! He'll probably respect and admire me for my forthright independence!"

Second, be assertive and a little dramatic with yourself. Half-hearted arguments won't work.

For example:

Irrational thought: "My children will think I'm terribly selfish if I ask to have some time to be left alone."
Ineffective argument: "It's probably my right, isn't it?"

Irrational thought: "If I call up my old friend Joe he probably won't even remember me."
Ineffective argument: "He might."

Third, don't argue with your arguments. You'll end up going around in circles like a dog chasing its tail. You'll probably get nowhere fast! Like this:

Irrational thought: "My daughter will probably hate me if I don't let her use the car whenever she wants."

Ineffective argument: "I have a right to say 'no'. On the other hand, her whining will be insufferable if I do. But it's my car and she won't even respect me unless I stand up for my rights. Yeah, but if I don't let her use the car, she'll stay around the house and make a terrible pain of herself because I wouldn't loan her the car."

Fourth, argue with your thoughts, *not with your emotion.* Some people call this "suppressing" your emotion. Such arguments are not only ineffective but potentially quite harmful. They don't assist you in changing your emotion — only in hiding it!

Irrational thought: "The least she could have done was wish me a happy anniversary. After all, we've only been married 38 years!"
Ineffective argument: "Don't get upset. It's silly to get angry."

Irrational thought: "This is the third time this week they've dropped off the grandchildren for me to babysit without asking. I guess they just don't care about me!"
Ineffective argument: "It's dumb to feel so hurt."

Attack those irrational thoughts until they no longer exist! Make your arguments as persuasive as possible. Use powerful arguments. "Shout" them in your head. And use several arguments for each irrational thought.

Here are some more appropriate arguments for the above irrational thoughts:

Irrational thought: "It's catastrophic that my girlfriend got angry with me."
Argument: "No, it's not! She's been this angry before and we were able to work it out. I've just got to be patient."

Irrational thought: "If I ask for vacation time now, my boss will probably think I'm a lazy good-for-nothing and will hate me."
Argument: "I've never seen him respond that way to anybody. Besides, I'm just mind-reading, based on absolutely no information! Furthermore, vacation time is my right, since I earned it, and I can ask for it any time I want to."

Irrational thought: "My children will think I'm terribly selfish if I ask to have some time to be left alone."
Argument: "I have a right to time alone. I can explain what I want in a nice way, and then how they feel is up to them! Anyway, I have no reason to believe that they will think I'm selfish."

Irrational thought: "If I call up my old friend Joe he probably won't even remember me."
Argument: "That's hardly likely! And even if he doesn't remember me at first, there's nothing wrong with refreshing his memory. I've got nothing to lose and a lot to gain!"

Irrational thought: "My daughter will probably hate me if I don't let her use the car whenever she wants."
Argument: (Same argument as before, but without counter-arguments.) "I have a right to say 'no.' It's *my* car and she won't respect me unless I stand up for my rights."

If you have difficulty thinking of arguments against an irrational thought, that usually means that the irrational thought is very strong. The best thing to do is to imagine how someone you respect, who does not have that irrational thought, would argue with you. If that isn't enough, actually ask them for some arguments against your irrational thought. If you are working on this with friends, try to help one another think of good arguments.

When you understand this concept thoroughly you will have one of the basic tools for the techniques I will soon describe. But before you read on make sure you can first construct good arguments against your irrational thoughts. Try out your skills on the following exercise:

Write two arguments against each irrational thought:

1. "Since my boss criticized me, that means I'm no good!"

_____

_____

2. "She looks like a very interesting person, but she probably wouldn't be interested in meeting me."

_____

_____

3. "I'd better not disagree with what they are saying, because then they might not like me."

_____

_____

4. "I'd better not acknowledge their compliments too readily, or I'll look self-centered."

_____

_____

5. "Even though the clerk short-changed me, I'm afraid he might think I'm trying to cheat him if I go back and tell him about it."

_____

_____

If you couldn't think of any of your own counters, you can steal some of mine:

1. _Irrational thought:_ "Since my boss criticized me, that means I'm no good!"

   Argument: "Wrong! All it means is that he doesn't like something I did. I may or may not benefit from his criticism, but there's no point in drawing dumb conclusions in any case!"

2. *Irrational thought:* "She looks like a very interesting person, but she probably wouldn't be interested in meeting me."

    Argument: "There's no way I'll know whether she's interested in meeting me unless I introduce myself. 'Nothing ventured, nothing gained!'"

3. *Irrational thought:* "I'd better not disagree with what they are saying, because they may not like me."

    Argument: "They can't like me unless they respect me, and they can't respect me unless I voice my own opinion. Anyway, it's *my* opinion, and I like it."

4. *Irrational thought:* "I'd better not acknowledge their compliments too readily, or I'll look self-centered."

    Argument: "If I don't thank them for their compliments, then they will be less likely to compliment me in the future. Since I deserve the compliments, there's nothing wrong with showing appreciation."

5. *Irrational thought:* "Even though the clerk short-changed me, I'm afraid he might think I'm trying to cheat him if I go back and tell him about it."

    Argument: "Nonsense! It's *my* money and I have a right to try to get it back, as long as I am courteous. Furthermore, I am trying to mind read, which is dumb."

CHAPTER 7

MIND TRICKS

Cognitive Exercises

Cognitive exercises are daily regimens involving thoughts and images. They all require that you close your eyes, relax and go through a series of prescribed steps.

The purpose of cognitive exercises is to teach skills in dealing with situations before the situations arise. This is sort of like ground school for pilots or dress rehearsal for actors. More specifically, these cognitive exercises teach you how to handle difficult situations with rational thinking — at times *other* than when the situations are actually occurring!

For example, let's suppose that you have a problem saying "no." Rather than waiting until such a situation arises, you can use the cognitive exercises to provide yourself with many opportunities to use this skill. You can learn at your own pace, without the pressure of a demanding situation. Then, when you do need to say "no," you can!

Another advantage of cognitive exercises is that they afford you lots of practice. They let you practice rational thinking over and over again, without your having to wait for the actual situation to occur. What would have otherwise taken years to learn can now be learned in weeks or days!

You will learn three cognitive exercises. Each exercise accomplishes a slightly different purpose. However, there are several important common elements.

First, as stated above, each one requires that you relax, close your eyes, and go through certain prescribed series of thoughts and images. You will find that your imagery is better if you lie down.

Second, each exercise requires extreme concentration. Letting your thoughts wander off the subject renders the whole exercise useless. If you are one of those individuals who cannot produce mental images, or cannot concentrate, then your best bet is to close your eyes and actually say the entire exercise out loud. Still, concentrate as best you can.

Third, each exercise requires that you use as many details and as much clarity in your imagery as possible. Use colors, smells, textures — whatever details you can supply. You should be aware that the longer a period of time you concentrate, the harder it is to keep all these details. That's okay. It means you're working as hard as you should be.

Practice Makes Rational

Sometimes irrational thinking feels much more comfortable than rational thinking. This is simply because you have practiced the irrational thought more often than you have practiced the rational thought.

The same is true of arguments against irrational thoughts. The arguments will seem uncomfortable and unnatural, while the irrational thoughts will feel like they fit you just fine!

Voluntary cortical inhibition (VCI) is designed to turn the tables. It will teach you, in a controlled practice situation, to argue quickly and naturally with irrational thoughts. In fact, it will get to the point that when you are in a tough situation you will find yourself arguing against the irrational thoughts automatically. Eventually the irrational thoughts won't even occur to you.

How to do it: If you have learned how to write your situations, thoughts, reactions and arguments, the VCI will be a snap! The first thing you will have to do is identify a situation in which you would like to feel or act differently from the way you do now. To start with, pick a situation about which you are only moderately bothered. I know the temptation will be to pick the worst situation you can think of, but *don't do it.* The chances of success are always greater if you start small and work your way up.

Close your eyes for a second. Imagine the situation and try to estimate how disturbing you find it. A good way to estimate is to use a zero to ten scale. Zero means no disturbance level and ten means the disturbance is awful. The situation you choose should have no greater a disturbance level than five or six. Later, when you've practiced a bit, you can go after the bigger ones. Now write the situation. You don't have to write more than a couple of sentences at most. But when you close your eyes later, you should be able to see the complete scene.

Next, write the irrational thought. Even though you may have more than one irrational thought about this situation, just write down the one you want to work on for now. And later, when your eyes are closed, just think about this one and don't think about any of the others. (When you have eliminated this irrational thought, you may want to use the same scene to work on others, one at a time).

Now write your reaction. Keep this to only a couple of words or so, just like you learned earlier.

For the last part, write at least four or five good arguments against the irrational thought. Make them as persuasive as possible.

Now you are ready. Lean back or (preferably) lie down. Take a few good deep breaths to relax yourself. Look very carefully at what you have written, then close your eyes. This will take three or four minutes of hard concentration, because you will run through the entire exercise *three times* before opening your eyes.

1. First imagine the situation in as much detail as possible. When the scene is clear.

2. imagine saying the irrational thought to yourself and

3. imagine how you feel and act. When you have done all this,

4. IMMEDIATELY argue with the irrational thought. When you run out of good arguments recycle the old ones and try to think of new ones. Be firm and imagine shouting the arguments to yourself. After about half a minute of this,

5. go back to the situation and start the whole process over again, until you have done it all a total of three times.

Then open your eyes and use the zero to ten scale to rate your progress. If you followed all of the directions, your **disturbance level should have dropped about two points**; however, it is not unusual for it to drop more than that.

Here's an example: *Situation;* I walk into the house after eight hours at the office. The house is in a shambles, as it was when I left this morning. Since this is a Saturday, my husband and kids have been home all day. *Thought:* "My husband and kids are terrible; they don't contribute to the household and they probably don't care!!" *Reaction:* I feel angry and start shouting. *Argument:* I need more information before I start making assumptions. I didn't make my expectations clear — in fact I didn't even voice them! They have all contributed plenty to the household, but if I want them to contribute housecleaning, I should negotiate that with them. (Whole exercise done three times before opening eyes).

As you practice this technique, you will get better at reducing the level of disturbing thoughts. Be aware, however, that for every two steps forward, you will take one step back. For example, if you reduced a thought from a level of five to a level of one, don't be surprised if tomorrow it's a two or three. For this reason, when you get a thought to a zero level, it is wise to keep working a while longer, so that in the future it will stay at the zero level.

Don't forget to start with situations which you find only moderately disturbing. If you have one situation in particular that you want to work on, but it's at level ten, then work up to it. For instance, let's say that you would like to ask your employer for a raise, but you find the very notion traumatizing. First, arrange a list of five to ten situations in which you have to ask for something. Range them from minimal disturbance (e.g., ask waitress for more coffee) all the way up to asking for a raise. Use this cognitive exercise to progress *upward* through the list. Each time you reduce a disturbance level to a one or a zero, then move to the next item on your list. Keep going through your list this way until you have conquered all of them, including the very last one: asking for a raise.

It is hard to say how many times per day you should use this technique. Ideally, I would say you should perform VCI (steps one through five, which means doing the situation-thought-reaction-argument cycle three times for each exercise) a total of five times per day. If you are attempting to eliminate a particularly troublesome thought, I would recommend more. In any case, do it as much as possible. See Appendix I for more sample arguments.

Self-Instruction Training

Half the battle is over when you conquer an irrational thought. The other half of the battle is in training yourself to think rationally.

Irrational thinking is no more of an accident than rational thinking. But until now you may have been "practicing" irrational thinking. In fact, you may have practiced it so well that some of your irrational thoughts seem "spontaneous." Now that you have learned how to defeat your irrational thinking, it's time to learn how to practice rational thinking until *it* becomes "spontaneous" instead.

A good technique for this is *Self-Instruction Training* (SIT). This is a cognitive exercise, like VCI. However, this exercise uses the principle of self-reinforcement of rational thinking. Specifically, SIT will help you learn to use rational *self-instructions* for situations in which you had previously thought irrationally. Of central importance is the "self-instruction." Self-instructions are instructions or directives that you give yourself. They direct you to act and/or feel a specified way.

Here are some examples of self-instructions:

Situation: You're at a party and see someone you don't know, but would like to.
Self-instruction: "I should introduce myself — I've got nothing to lose."
Reaction: Confident; introduces self.

Situation: You come home from work and your kids don't give you any attention.
Self-instruction: "Since I want attention, I should ask for it."
Reaction: Calm, ask for attention.

Situation: Your children are playing quietly together.
Self-instruction: "Catch them being good."
Reaction: Compliment them.

Situation: Your sister makes a statement you disagree with.
Self-instruction: "Speak Up!"
Reaction: Disagree.

Situation: Your boy friend does not return from ski trip in time for important date.
Self-instruction: "Wait and get more information."
Reaction: Wait to ask why.

Notice that each self-instruction gives clear directions. Also notice that each is worded broadly enough that the same exact words could be used in similar situations. For instance, there are many situations in which your children are behaving nicely and you could remember to compliment them by reminding yourself to "catch them being good." And surely there are many situations in which people have broken agreements, and you would do well to "wait and get more information." (Incidentally, you may have observed that some of the self-instructions would make good arguments against irrational thoughts.)

SIT, like VCI, requires you to relax, close your eyes and go through certain prescribed steps in your thinking. Those steps were alluded to above: *situation, self-instruction, reaction.*

Self-instructions are explained above.

Here are some hints on the other two components, situation and reaction:

Situation: Imagine the situation as clearly and vividly as you can. These should be situations in which you have conquered your irrational thoughts and would now like to insert rational thinking. For the purposes of the exercise, the situations may be experiences you have really had or just situations you made up for the exercise. From day to day as you practice SIT, vary the situations used for the same self-instruction.

Reaction: Imagine following your self-instruction. And imagine feeling good as you do it. *How* you feel good may vary from one situation to another. You may feel calm, competent, confident, loved, enthusiastic, or anything else that feels good!

When you do SIT, you should:

1. Sit back or (preferably) lie down, close your eyes and relax.

2. Like a movie camera, without emotion, imagine the situation clearly.

3. Then imagine very explicitly saying the self-instruction to yourself. (Remember, just the instruction. No irrational thoughts).

4. Imagine calmly, confidently following your self-instructions.

5. Repeat this five times before opening your eyes.

Keep using this same self-instruction during your exercises until you find yourself using it automatically in real life. This usually occurs within a week or two if you practice frequently. A good regimen to follow is four complete sets every day. (See Appendix II for more sample self-instructions).

Covert Modeling

Sometimes the best way to learn assertion skills is by watching other people act assertively. The term for this type of learning is "modeling" — watching someone who is successful and copying their behavior.

When you have a specific goal in mind, this may be an inconvenient method to use. For instance, if your goal is to be able to say "no" to your mother-in-law, you could kill a lot of time waiting around, hoping to see someone say "no" to their own mother-in-law.

A nice alternative to this technique is "covert modeling." In this context "covert" simply means "in your head." Like the other cognitive exercises, it requires closing your eyes and, ideally, lying down.

Covert modeling involves imagining someone other than yourself (the "model") handling a situation assertively. You will learn best if you change the identity of the model from time to time.

Another pointer here is to follow the "small steps rule": imagine your model handling the situation assertively, but not so much better than you that it seems unrealistic. Later, when your behavior gets better, you should imagine a more ambitious model. Let's say that the goal you have set for yourself is: "Be able to return merchandise to stores, and feel comfortable doing so." And let's further assume that you have always had a very hard time doing this sort of thing. If you were following the small steps rule, your first image might go something like this:

In the men's wear department. You can see the color of the rug. You see all the merchandise counters and hear the bland background music. The hero walks up to the sales counter.

Hero: Pardon me . . . ahem. Pardon me.

Clerk: You want something?

Hero: Well, yes. Or actually, I don't want something. Ha ha. I would like to return some merchandise.

Clerk: (Looks annoyed.) Have your receipt?

Hero: Huh?

Clerk: You gotta have a receipt or you can't get a refund. Excuse me, I got a customer. (Clerk walks off. In a few minutes he's back.)

Hero: Pardon me. I found my receipt. (Hands clerk the receipt.)

Clerk: It looks like you bought this almost six weeks ago.

Hero: That's right. I bought it for my vacation, but when I got there I found that the shirt was mislabeled. I just got back from my vacation yesterday, so this was my first chance to return it.

Clerk: You can't return anything that was bought over 30 days ago. Sorry (Starts to turn around.)

Hero: (Blurts out) Then I'd like to see the department manager. Maybe he can make an exception.

Clerk: I've never seen him make an exception.

Hero: (Looking a little nervous.) I'd like to see him anyway.

Clerk: I don't know if he's in the store right now.

Hero: I'm really sorry to be such a bother, but I'd appreciate it if you could try to find him for me. (Clerk walks off, grumbling. Comes back shortly with older man).

Manager: May I help you, sir?

Hero: I really don't mean to be such a bother, but I bought this shirt here for my vacation. When I got there I found that the size had been mislabeled. I just got back from my vacation yesterday, but the purchase was made six weeks ago. Can you help me?

Manager: Well, we normally don't permit returns on items which have been out of the store for over 30 days.

Hero: I know, but I would appreciate an exception. Particularly in view of my circumstances and the fact that the shirt was mislabeled.

Manager: Okay. (To clerk.) Make out a refund slip for this gentleman.

He succeeded. Not brilliantly, not confidently, but he succeeded. When your behavior is as good as that of your models, then revise your models' behavior to make it even more assertive. The following example would reflect such a revision:

Hero: (Calm, courteous, good posture.) May I have a little of your time?

Clerk: You want something?

Hero: Yes. I'd like to return a shirt that doesn't fit me.

Clerk: You got a receipt?

Hero: I think it's in the sack — yes, here we go. (Hands it to clerk.)

Clerk: Looks like you bought this over six weeks ago.

Hero: (Courteous, unperturbed.) That's right.

Clerk: Well, you can't return anything that was bought over 30 days ago. It's against store rules.

Hero: That may be so, but I think my situation calls for an exception. I bought this shirt here for my vacation. When I tried it on, I discovered that the shirt size had been mislabeled. Since I was nowhere near one of your stores, I could not return it then. I just got back from vacation yesterday, so this is my first chance to bring it back.

Clerk: Yeah, but it's against the rules.

Hero: In that case, I'd like to see the department manager.

Clerk: I've never seen him make an exception to the rule.

Hero: That's okay. I'd like to see him anyway.

Clerk: I don't know if he's in the store right now.

Hero: I'd like you to try to find him in case he is in the store.

Clerk: Yeah, (Walks off grumbling.) (Clerk returns with older man.)

Manager: May I help you?

Hero: Yes. I would like to return a shirt that I bought here six weeks ago. I know that you do not normally accept returns on items that have been out of the store for over 30 days, but I think this may be a special situation. I bought the shirt for my vacation. When I tried it on, I discovered that the shirt size had been mislabeled and I was miles from any of your stores. Today is the first opportunity I've had to return it. Do think you think you can help me?

Manager: Well, actually it's against the rules.

Hero: Yes, I know. But I think you should make an exception, especially in view of the fact that I am having to return it because of a factory mistake.

Manager: Okay. (To clerk.) Make out a refund slip for this gentleman.

He succeeded, too. Smoothly, calmly, competently. Once you achieved these behaviors, it would probably be unnecessary to aim for anything more ambitious.

Although I have given examples for only two steps, you may find it useful to use only one step. Or it may be more realistic for you to use more than two steps. In any case, move in small comfortable increments.

Like the other cognitive exercises, covert modeling is best done regularly; spend five or ten minutes each day, working on one situation at a time. I suggest that you set aside a regular time each day so that it becomes part of your routine.

CHAPTER 8

GETTING THE MESSAGE ACROSS

You Don't Like Dishonest Questions, Do You?

Now why would anyone ask you a question that has only one right answer?

Look at those two questions above and you will see that they are both pointless. And, that's the point.

Some questions are unassertive and indirect attempts to communicate. Here are some examples of what I mean:

Questions with no Options

To a two-year-old child: "Do you want to go to bed now?"

To a twelve-year-old: "Do you want to help Dad with the yard work?"

To your wife: "I've invited my folks over for dinner tonight. Do you mind?"

To your boyfriend: "I've decided to go to the beach for the weekend. I'll have to break our date. Is that okay with you?"

Chances are that the expected answer to all of these questions is a form of "yes." Unless the person being asked is truly given the right to say "no," the question is dishonest. When there is no option (as in the case of the children), don't act as though there is. Make a statement of your expectations: "It is time for you to go to bed now." "I would like you to go help Dad with the yard work." Both of these statements communicate that there is a command, not a choice.

In the case of the wife and boyfriend, it is too late to permit a choice. A decision was made that involved them, but they are given no opportunity to state their desires. The person asking the question is, more accurately, expecting the acquiescence of the wife and boyfriend.

Questions as Punishers

"Why do you always stay up late when you know you have to get up early the next day?" "Why don't you ever do anything nice for me?" "Why do you always act as though you are the only one that counts around here?" "Why do you always want to hurt my feelings?"

Clearly, there are no right answers to these questions. They are designed to punish, not to communicate. The honest way to communicate dissatisfaction is to make a statement voicing the problem and a possible solution of the problem.

Instead of asking someone why they stay up late, ignore the situation and let them deal with it. Your attempts to punish such behavior are apt to have little effect. The natural consequence, having to function with little sleep, is more likely to bring about change.

There is no way someone can explain why they don't do nice things for you, so don't ask them to. Ask instead for what you want. You might say, "I would like it if you would occasionally do something that is just for me — like breakfast in bed or washing my back."

When it appears that another person does not have regard for the feelings of others, say "I would like for you to ask my opinion about our budget before you make decisions. It is important to me to have a chance to verbalize my thoughts."

When your feelings are hurt, let the other person know why. You could say, "I would like for you to talk to me in a quieter tone of voice. I feel hurt when you yell at me. Please don't do it."

Questions for the Wishy-Washy

"Boy, I really liked the movie — didn't you?" "He's a very nice person — don't you think?" "I think it would be a good idea for me to change schools, don't you?"

The person who asks questions such as these is making a statement and then standing ready to change his opinion if it is not substantiated by others.

If you answered the first question by saying "No, I didn't care for the movie. I thought the characters lacked pizazz," it would not be surprising for the person who asked the question to respond, "Yeah, you're right about that. I didn't really know what was wrong. But you're right, the characters lacked pizazz."

An assertive replacement for the first question would be, "I really liked the movie. How did you like it?" In this case a statement is made and a question is asked. It sounds much more assertive than simply tacking a question on to the tail end of a statement.

When the opinion of another person is sought for the purpose of decision making, come right out and say so. Say, "I'm trying to decide what to do about school. I'd like your input." What you want is very clear. You are not hiding behind the guise of having made the decision and casually seeking validation.

Questions with no options, questions as punishers, and questions for the wishy-washy are ineffective ways to communicate what you mean.

Questions with no options are an invitation to a hassle. Some people actually think they have the right to say "no," and find out too late they didn't.

Questions as punishers act as barriers to communication. The person being punished will either shut up or put up. Neither alternative deals with the problem at hand.

Questions for the wishy-washy are cop-outs for making decisive statements. If you think something, say it. If you want something, ask for it directly.

Look at your own behaviors. Can you hear yourself asking the type of questions that fall into these categories?

Questions with no options: _____

_____

_____

Questions as punishers: _____

_____

_____

Questions for the wishy-washy: _____

_____

_____

There is another type of question, one that you should be aware of because it is the pinnacle of subtle manipulation. This type of question is a favorite trick of people who have something to sell, be it goods, service or a belief.

Questions That Assume a Premise

"Don't you care enough about me to call every weekend?"
(Assumes that the only way to demonstrate caring is to make
a weekly phone call.)

"Don't you think enough of yourself to get a divorce?"
(Assumes that you can't like yourself and stay married.)

"When are you going to stop flirting with the devil and start
going to church?" (Assumes that not going to church
constitutes flirting with the devil.)

"Are you woman enough to keep your man?" (Assumes a
relationship between womanliness and "keeping" a man.)

"Isn't your kids' education important enough to you to buy
them this set of encyclopedias?" (Assumes that unless you
buy the encyclopedias you aren't interested in your kids'
education.)

"When are you going to show your love of country and get
actively involved in politics?" (Assumes that the only way to
show love of country is be active in politics.)

You can respond to this type of question by first questioning
the premise, then stating your position. You might say, "I do
care for you. The fact that I do not call you every weekend
means only that I do not call you every weekend. It does not
mean that I do not care for you."

On the next question, you could respond by saying, "I do
care for myself. However, I have not chosen divorce as a way
of expressing this."

The encyclopedia salesman could be told, "I am interested in
my children's education. I am not interested in buying your
encyclopedias."

See if you can think of questions which fall into this category
of questions that assume a premise:

_____

_____

_____

Messages Without Words

Your opinion of yourself shows. The way you carry yourself, the way you walk, and the way you sit all seem to reflect a general attitude you have about yourself.

Maybe you have noticed that on days when you are feeling "down," you walk differently than you do on your "up" days. Or perhaps you have noticed that you sit with your head down and your eyes focused on your hands when you are in a situation in which you feel shy. This behavior may be quite the opposite of the way you handle yourself in a business situation in which you feel confident and successful. Others interpret this language the body speaks. Because they do, it is important that you learn to convey the same message with your body as you do with your words.

Body Expression

Unassertive. Rounded shoulders, head down, eyes downcast, tightly clasped hands, a slow shuffle-type walk, lack of hand gestures, fiddling with your hair, face, pencil, etc. and sticking your fingers in your mouth.

Assertive. Straight shoulders, head erect, relaxed arms and hands, a steady, direct stride, straight posture, the use of hand gestures, and responsive nod of head.

Facial Expression

Unassertive. Darting, wandering eye movement, stiff lips, infrequent smiles, smiling while speaking seriously, staring off into space, stone face, worried face, tight lipped smile, covering your mouth with hand while smiling, biting your lip, excessive licking of lips, and moving your tongue a lot when you're not talking.

Assertive. A ready smile, looking directly at others during conversation, relaxed mouth and face, and facial expression matching verbal expression.

Some other things to consider are:

Distance

It is said that you should stand the appropriate distance from your (conversational) partner. This means you should not stand too close, but you should also not stand too far away. There are no absolutes here, but generally speaking people are comfortable when they are standing at handshake distance.

Touching

A touch on the shoulder, arm or hand is usually acceptable. It is better to touch others only occasionally during a conversation than it is to touch often.

As you begin to incorporate assertive body language you will find that you are able to communicate more effectively. It will become easier for you to convey your verbal message when your body is speaking the same language.

It's the Way You Say It

An assertive verbal response is more than just words — it's the *way* you say the words. Almost any message could be construed as passive, assertive, or aggressive depending on the way you say it. Here are some things to look for:

Voice Quality

Unassertive. Speaking in monotone, making a statement but raising your voice at the end as though you had asked a question, beginning sentences in clear voice but fizzling out the tail end words, small, barely audible voice, loud blaring voice, an accusing tone of voice, an "it really doesn't matter to me" tone of voice, and a whining tone of voice.

Assertive: Speaking in well-modulated tone of voice, that is, you add different tones to emphasize meanings; making a direct statement and bringing it to a clear, concise ending; and a firm positive tone of voice.

Fluency

Unassertive. Umm, you know okay? right? like, sort of, kind of, and well-uh are all words which interfere with fluency. Giggling, a nervous laugh, clearing throat frequently, and starting sentences and not finishing them are all behaviors which interfere with fluency.

Assertive. Flowing presentation of statements, no extraneous words and sounds, and expressing complete thoughts.

You may choose to get feedback via a tape recorder or friends to find out where you might make changes. Once you are aware of what you are doing that sounds unassertive, you can use counting and recording as a method to change your behavior.

Choice of Words

Rational thinking leads to rational behavior. However, when you are first changing from irrational to rational thinking, you may be temporarily left speechless: You simply may not know what to say. In this exercise, I would like you to learn to identify assertive responses, write out your own assertive responses, and use covert modeling to practice your assertive responses. First, I will take you through some examples of various responses and ask you to pick out the assertive ones.

Pick the assertive responses: (Answers follow exercise)

1. I asked you nicely, so I don't see why you have to say "no" to my request.
2. Your behavior makes me very unhappy.
3. Would you please be more specific about what I did that you didn't like?
4. I don't see why you always have to do it your way.
5. Why can't you ever be on time?
6. I like it very much when you say "I love you." I would like it very much if you said it more often.
7. I have feelings, too, you know.
8. I can't stand it when you leave dishes in the living room.
9. It's not fair that you get to sleep in when I have to get up and go to work.
10. I would like us to share the responsibility of the housework.

Answers:

1. Unassertive. *Asking* for what you want gives the other person the right to say "yes" or "no." Extending rights to others is as important as your standing up for your own rights. If you are disappointed at the other person's response, you might say, "I am disappointed."

2. Unassertive. You are giving the other person responsibility for the way you feel. You can say, "I feel unhappy about what you did."

3. Assertive! This is a good response to use when someone makes a general accusation regarding your behavior.

80

4. Unassertive. When someone else always has it his way, you are giving in to his wishes. Don't *blame* him, but do *accept* the responsibility for standing up for what you want. You could say, "I would rather go to a play since we have been to several movies lately." If your partner does not care to do what you want, and *insists* you come along to another movie, *decide* whether you want to go.

5. Unassertive. This is a dishonest question, and a punishing one at that. If you wish to let the other person know you want him to be on time, say so. You can say, "I would appreciate your making an effort to be on time. I dislike having to wait."

6. Assertive. You reinforced the behavior you liked and asked for what you want.

7. Unassertive. You are not asking for what you want, which is for consideration. You can say, "I would appreciate your consideration of my feelings. This is important to me."

8. Unassertive. Obviously you can stand it. The dishes are there and you are surviving in spite of it. If you would like someone to do something, ask for it. "Would you please put the dishes in the dishwasher?" is a direct request.

9. Unassertive. This world is not fair. This statement sounds as though you are picking a fight. It is doubtful the other person would have the least idea of your expectations.

10. Assertive. Notice you asked for "sharing" of housework, not "help" with housework.

That was just your side of it. What if you are assertive and the other person responds aggressively or passively? Well, that "what if?" is a real possibility and you can prepare yourself to deal with it. Let's look at some discussions between two people.

You have just told your girl friend that you would prefer she not make plans for you. When someone invites the two of you to do something, you want her to check with you before accepting the invitation. She replies by saying, "I don't like it when you act that way." Always before, you apologized for acting "that way" without really knowing what her criticism was. This time you say, "Would you please be more specific about what I did that you didn't like. She replies, "Oh, you know what I don't like. Don't play innocent with me." You respond by saying, "I'm not really sure what you think I did wrong. I'm asking you to be more specific. I can't agree or disagree with you until I know the exact problem. "

She says, "You were acting like you don't care about my feelings; I can't even tell someone we'll go some place with them until I ask you. That's a real nuisance. I think you're doing that to get back at me for something." You calmly respond by saying, "I do care about your feelings, but I also care about mine. Often times I have ended up going places with people I would rather not be with. I don't want to do that any more. I know it's an extra bother to you to ask me, but that's what I want you to do for me. I'm asking you to consider my rights in making plans. I'm not trying to get back at you; you've done nothing wrong."

Even though she was upset, you responded calmly and without criticism of her behavior. You stuck to your goal of stating your desires. You were not distracted by her accusations that you were purposely trying to hurt her. You were empathetic and yet firm.

Your wife is one to take you "for granted." She does many nice things for you and is, in general, thoughtful and responsive. However, she does not verbalize her feelings to you. When you tell her, "I love you," she usually says, "I love you, too." You would like for her to initiate saying "I love you." You tell her, "I like it very much when you say "I love you." I would like to have you say it even more often."

She responds by saying, "I tell you I love you! But I guess you wouldn't know that since you never listen to me. While you're complaining, you might as well tell me what else you don't like about me."

Although she was upset and snide, you decide not to let it get to you. You say, "I know you tell me that you love me. It's just that you usually say it to me only when I say it first. It would be nice if you were just to come up to me and say it first. I know you say it already, that's how I know I like it. I'm sorry you think I'm complaining about you. It is not my intention to complain, but to let you know what I want. I love you very much and I'll try always to let you know when there's a problem — the only problem we have now, though, is to get this little matter clear between us."

You did not back off in attempting to make yourself clear. Although your wife became defensive, you did not apologize for what you wanted in an effort to make her feel at ease.

You were reassuring and reinforcing — and direct.

You have a friend come to visit you from out of town. The visit was to last a week, but due to circumstances, will be extended to two months. You did not expect any help with housework while your friend was a visitor, but wish to establish some new ground rules for the extended living together situation. You say, "Since you will be here, not as a guest, but as a housemate, I would like us to share the responsibility for the housework." Your friend replies, "Well! If you don't want me here, all you have to do is say so! I'm beginning to get the idea you are trying to get rid of me. If you didn't want me to stay you should have said so."

Your friend is reading a lot into what you said. Even though you made a seemingly direct statement, your friend mistook it for an indirect one. You can say, "Hey, I want you here. That's why I invited you to stay with me. I like being with you. It's just that I thought we ought to work out a system for living together with the least amount of friction. I thought it best we get the housekeeping stuff worked out first. If there's something you want to ask of me, feel free to speak up."

You directly responded to everything your friend said. You did not label his behavior, nor make accusations. You simply persevered with stating your request. No blame was placed for the misunderstanding.

You are involved in a discussion with a group of people at a cocktail party. Someone states a rather lengthy, detailed opinion about something. You didn't quite catch it all, and say, "I don't understand. Would you please repeat your last point?" The speaker replies by saying, "I'm sorry. Sure didn't mean to offend you. I didn't know where you stood on this issue. Hey, I'm really sorry if I said something wrong."

Although the speaker was unnecessarily defensive, you do not attack his behavior. You say, "No problem. I honestly didn't understand what you said."

The speaker may be too embarrassed at this point to continue this discussion. If so, you may elect to simply drop it and bring up a new topic or join another group.

Now, you do it. Think of all the situations you wish to handle more assertively. Start with situations involving low risk relationships. Use only the situations about which you now have rational thoughts.

And remember. This is not your chance to get back at the world. It is your chance to learn to speak more assertively.

If you are unable to come up with something different to say, it may be because you haven't gotten rid of all your irrational thoughts about the situation. Go back to the use of VCI if necessary. Then try this exercise again.

CHAPTER 9
PRINCIPLES OF LEARNING

If you're like almost everybody else, you probably find yourself wondering "why" about your own behaviors and emotions as well as about the behaviors and emotions of others. The "why" is often presumed to be a question of motivation — "Why did I do that?" "Why did he say that to me?" "Why does she get depressed so often?" "Why do others treat me the way they do?"

When you ask such questions, it is probably your desire to hit upon something that will explain the behavior. You might even hope that once you know "why," you will be enlightened and, hence, have the ability to change your behavior or to better understand and accept the behavior of others.

Often the answers you get do not promote change or understanding. Perhaps this is because you asked the wrong question.

Consider asking questions such as:

How was the behavior learned?
Why does the behavior continue?
How can I learn new behaviors?
How can I teach new behaviors?
How can I solve the problem?

In order to answer these questions you may need to know more about the process of learning. If you want to know more about learning, then please read on, because I'd love to teach you!

The principles of learning are the same for everyone. Some very predictable things happen during the learning process. These natural laws of learning are obeyed by everyone. Your own knowledge of these principles makes learning, teaching and changing more efficient.

Positive Reinforcement

An event or object which follows a behavior and *increases* the chances of the behavior occurring again.

This is the best operational definition of *Positive Reinforcer,* but there is another definition that is just about as good: If it felt good once, you'll probably do it again.

These are some of the things which are often positively reinforcing to people:

Smile	Breakfast in bed	Sleeping
Hug	Reading	Touch
Kiss	Movies	Money
Eye Contact	A foot massage	Praise
Kind words	I love you	Wink
Privilege	Playing outdoors	Being with friends
Cake	Talking	Television
Laugh	Music	Using a skill
Making love	Learning	

Nothing on this list is a "guaranteed" positive reinforcer. Most of the things mentioned are reinforcing, most of the time. But what is reinforcing at one time, may not be at another. What is reinforcing to one person may be embarrassing to another (such as a hug).

In order to determine whether you are being effective in changing or teaching a behavior, look at the results. Forget about what you *intended*— just look at what you got. If the behavior is increasing, it's being reinforced.

Here are some examples of the use of positive reinforcement. You come home from work and your partner greets you with, "Hi, it's so good to see you. I thought about you all day."

Your kid mows the lawn. You say "thank you" and offer the privilege of using the family car. Your kid says "thanks."

You calmly express to your friend your dissatisfaction with something he did. He replies, "I'm sorry you're not happy about what happened. I sure do appreciate your letting me know. That was really assertive!"

You walk over to a friend's house to give her a book. She gives you a foot massage.

You smile at a stranger. She smiles back.

You paint a picture. Everyone praises you for your talent.

You express your feelings of loving and caring to your partner. Next morning, you receive breakfast in bed with the comment, "I love the way you have been more open with me. Thank you."

In each of these examples the behaviors were followed with something pleasant. You are likely to repeat those behaviors (or behaviors very much like them). You have been *positively reinforced* for each thing you did. In most examples, the other person was also positively reinforced. Your partner was reinforced when you came home. The kid got reinforced with "thank you" and the car. The friend got reinforced with the book. The stranger was reinforced with your smile. Your partner was reinforced by your expression of positive feelings. In all cases, the interaction was mutually satisfying.

Some ringers: The things you least suspect as positive reinforcers are frequently positively reinforcing.

Things such as:

Spanking	Scolding	Alone in room
Yelling	Lecturing	Arguing

Many children, for instance, get no attention for desirable behavior but get spankings for undesirable behavior. In such cases spankings become the only form of attention from the parents. The child learns to behave in ways that get him this attention.

Some people learn that the only time their spouse talks to them is during an argument. For them there is a desire to talk and an absence of ordinary conversation; arguing is the closest they can come to getting what they want.

If you or someone you live with has an unwanted behavior, look for what happens following that behavior. You may find that the unwanted behavior is inadvertently being reinforced.

Untidiness is a behavior that is often reinforced unintentionally. Here's what happens: Your roommate leaves her clothes strewn about the apartment all the time. You have assertively requested she pick up her clothes, but she leaves them out any way. Because you like the apartment to be tidy, you end up picking up after your roommate. You might even hope your roommate will be embarrassed that you picked up after her. You hope the embarrassment will be enough to teach her to pick up her own things.

But let's look at the results — not your intentions. She left her clothes strewn about, but you picked them up. She once again left her clothes about, you once again picked them up. This goes on and on. You keep asking her to pick up her clothes and she keeps on leaving them strewn about.

Obviously, you did not "teach" her a lesson. Not as obviously, you are reinforcing her by doing her work for her. Oops!

Procrastination also gets reinforced a lot. Your spouse agrees to write the checks to pay the bills. A week goes by, still the checks are not written. You constantly remind "spouse" to write checks; yet another week goes by and still the checks are not written. Finally, you give in and write the checks.

Let's go so far as to say this goes on every month around your house. You constantly remind that the checks are to be written, but they never get written until you do it yourself. Procrastination pays off well for your spouse. You do all the work. Your giving in and doing the job inadvertently reinforces the procrastination of your spouse.

Poor work is another behavior that is often accidentally reinforced. One sure way to get out of having to do the job again is to do it poorly the first time. Kids learn early how to avoid work. Since parents do not always care to invest the time in teaching the kid to do the job correctly, and since the kid doesn't automatically do it correctly, the parent ends up doing it. Of course, the parent also ends up feeling resentful if the kid doesn't help.

The pattern here is: kid does poor job, so parent ends up doing the job. Give the kid yet another job to do, it is done poorly, so parent does it. This could go on and on. Pretty soon, the parent may even give up asking for help and just do everything alone.

Sickness is a behavior that is often reinforced. Lots of tender, loving care is given to the person who is ill. Too often, as soon as the illness has subsided, the loving attention is withdrawn. Others find themselves "too busy" to give members of their family special attention — unless there is a crisis of some sort.

At our home we have arranged with each other to ask to be pampered. Instead of announcing that "I am ill today and can't go to work," I announce that "Today I am taking the day off. Anything you care to do to pamper me will be appreciated." The person taking the day off gets a lot of special attention. Plus, it is easier for other family members — the person taking the day off is having a good time, instead of complaining about aches and pains.

In the following examples people are getting reinforced for appropriate as well as inappropriate behaviors. What behavior is being reinforced and who or what is reinforcing it? See end of exercise for answers.

1. Julie cries, "I can't do it, Daddy." So Daddy picks Julie up and says, "Don't cry, sweetheart. Daddy will fix it."

2. George comes home from work. Marge asks, "How was your day, dear?" "It was awful," George replies. Long silence, no further conversation until George says, "I had a very good talk with David today. First chance we've had to get together in a long time." "I'm glad for you, dear." Conversation stops once again until George says, "You know, I can't see why David puts up with that wife of his. Why I wouldn't be married to her for 15 minutes." Marge's ears pick up and she says, "Oh, really. What did she do? Why don't you like her?" George and Marge sit down for the next 20 minutes discussing the faults of David's wife.

3. Glenda calls to Susan, "Will you come help me clean up the kitchen, please?" Susan responds, "Sure thing. Be right there." Susan comes into the kitchen and says to Glenda, "Thanks for letting me know you wanted help."

4. Whenever Bobby pouts and tells his mother she hurt his feelings, his mother apologizes and tells him, "Mommy will buy you a new toy so you won't feel bad any more."

5. Lu explains to her sister, Mary, she would like Mary to ask to borrow her clothing rather than just take it. Mary replies, "Gosh, Lu, I didn't know it mattered to you." Lu replies, "Well, it really does bother me to find something missing when I want to wear it." Mary answers, "I just never thought about it that way. No problem. Next time I'll ask."

6. Pat recently met a man at a party. She very much enjoyed his company and conversation, and wished to pursue getting to know him. She suggested they get together one day for lunch and he accepted.

7. Mike, an artist, was asked to do some art work — without pay — for an acquaintance. Mike declined to work for no pay, and explained his fee schedule. The acquaintance commended Mike for his straightforward way of handling the situation.

8. Doris' mother asked Doris to take her shopping. She wanted to leave within the next hour. Doris told her mother she would not be able to drive her today, but could drive her

tomorrow. Her mother accepted the alternative.

9. Chris decided to write to the authors of a book she enjoyed and request they hire her to to translate the book into Spanish. She sent the authors a sample translation and they hired her to do the translation.

10. Chuck moved into his own apartment shortly after he turned 18. His family and friends threw a housewarming party for him.

11. Vickie has been told by many of her friends that they dislike her lateness in keeping appointments. They threatened to go off without her if she were not on time, but she continued to arrive late and they continued to wait for her.

12. Robert called a close woman friend and told her that he needed to talk to her. Could he come over then? She told him she was too busy to see him. A couple of hours later he called back and said he *must* talk to her immediately because he thought he might commit suicide. She told him to come over immediately and that she wanted to help him in any way she could.

13. Ethel has seven grown children. Some live nearby and others live in distant places. It is a rare occasion any of her children visit her. Ethel became ill and had to be hospitalized. All of her children visited her during her days of hospitalization.

14. Beth is a dedicated, efficient employee. Each year she receives healthy merit raises from her employer. Her supervisor often praises her for her high quality work.

15. John is a robust senior citizen. He plays in a band, takes classes at the local college, and runs two miles a day. Many of his younger acquaintances tell him they admire him for his vigor and enthusiasm for life. His peers respect him for his sharp wit and physical stamina.

16. Whenever Tom does odd jobs and repairs at his own home, no one ever seems to notice. He has found that he would rather help his parents out around their house than work at home. His parents are extremely grateful for the time he spends with them and occasionally give him an extra $20 to spend on himself.

17. Carla, a recent divorcee, has become quite timid on her job. She feels terribly insecure on her job. She is also

becoming increasingly dissatisfied with her job, because her boss has been giving her more and more work to do. Although she has not told her boss, she has been having to come in early and stay late in order to keep all her work caught up. She wishes she did not have so much extra work.

18. Don decided to give up eating bread and pastries. He also quit eating second helpings at meal time. In one month he lost 10 pounds.

19. Carol and David have a beautifully furnished home and they wear lovely clothes. All their friends admire their possessions. The only problem is Carol and David don't have any money — everything they have was bought on credit.

20. Jake is a great teacher. He is an exuberant person and has the ability to involve his students in projects. His classes are always well attended and assignments by students completed. Students often thank him for getting them involved in his subject.

Answers:

1. Since Julie was doing two things at the same time (crying and saying "I can't"), both behaviors were reinforced by Dad's picking her up and consoling her.

2. George did not get reinforced by Marge for having a good day or a fine time with an old friend. He did get reinforced by her for gossiping about another woman.

3. Glenda got reinforced by Susan's agreeing to help and also by Susan's statement of "thanks".

4. Bobby's mother reinforced his pouting and "you hurt my feelings" accusation when she apologized and when she promised him a toy.

5. Lu was reinforced by Mary for asking for what she wanted. If Mary does what she agreed to do (ask before taking clothes), Lu is further reinforced by Mary.

6. Pat was reinforced for asking a man out by his acceptance.

7. Mike was reinforced for refusing to work without pay. The acquaintance's comment about Mike's straightforward behavior was reinforcing.

8. Doris was reinforced for standing up for what *she* wanted. Her mother's acceptance of the alternative plan was reinforcing.

9. Chris wanted something and invested some time and energy toward getting it. She was reinforced by being accepted by the authors.

10. Chuck's independence was celebrated and thereby reinforced by friends and family.

11. Vickie's lateness was reinforced by friends and family.

12. Robert's threat to commit suicide was reinforced by his woman friend agreeing to see him only then.

13. Ethel was reinforced by her children for being ill and hospitalized.

14. Beth is reinforced with praise and monetary rewards for a job well done.

15. John receives a variety of reinforcement from a variety of people for being active and alert in his old age.

16. Tom receives "thank you" and money from his parents for being helpful. Even though the work itself may have been reinforcing to Tom, it became additionally reinforcing only at his parents' home.

17. Carla is accidentally reinforcing her boss for giving her extra work. She is getting all the work done at no extra expense to him (and no complaining from her).

18. Don was reinforced for changing his eating behavior. Weight loss was the payoff.

19. Carol and David were reinforced for spending more than they could afford. They had nice things immediately and they had the praise of their friends.

20. Jake is reinforced for being a good teacher. The attendance, completed assignments, and thanks from his students are all reinforcing.

Ah, as we all know, life is not simple. But even the complexities of life follow simple rules. You have just learned about one simple rule (positive reinforcement) of learning theory. Now for another rule: *Negative Reinforcement*.

Negative Reinforcement

The termination of a stimulus following a behavior which *increases* the chances of the behavior occurring again.

The way to define it is if that behavior brought you some relief in the situation, you'll probably use the behavior again in that situation.

You've heard the old saying, "it feels so good when it quits hurting." Well, negative reinforcement is very much like the old saying. Look at the examples.

These events are *generally* negative reinforcing to people:

Stop yelling	Stop the noise	Stop lecturing
Stop complaining	Stop the pain	Stop hitting
Stop pestering	Stop nagging	Stop threatening
Stop putting down	Stop punishing	Stop begging
Stop calling names	Stop poking	Stop intimidating
Stop hassling		

The similarity between positive and negative reinforcement is both serve to strengthen the behaviors they follow. When a behavior is positively or negatively reinforced, the behavior is likely to be repeated.

Here are some examples of negative reinforcement:

You are extremely nervous. You take a Valium and you are soon calm. (The behavior of taking Valium was reinforced by your subsequently feeling calm.)

You turn on the ignition of your car. A buzzer goes off. You fasten your seat belt and the buzzing stops. (The behavior of fastening your seat belt is reinforced by the discontinuance of noise.)

Are you beginning to notice the difference between positive and negative reinforcement? Look at both lists. Notice that the list of positive reinforcers are all things that are *added to* (given) the environment following the behavior. And on the list of negatively reinforcing events, something was *taken away* (stopped) from the environment following the behavior.

Look closely at yet some more examples.

Another kid hits you and twists your arm until you cry "uncle." As soon as you give in and cry "uncle," the hurting and twisting stop. (The behavior of giving in is reinforced by the cessation of pain.)

Your father yells at you about anything and everything until you go to bed. As soon as you go to bed he stops yelling. (Your behavior of going to bed terminates the yelling. Your behavior of going to bed is reinforced by quietness.)

Your child pokes you on the shoulder and cries, "Mommy, Mommy, Mommy." This keeps you until you finally give in and impatiently tell the child to quit bothering you while you're talking. The child immediately stops. (Your behavior of telling the child to stop was reinforced by the subsequent termination of poking and interrupting.)

Your boss asks you to stay late and finish a project. You refuse, politely. Your boss does not take "no" for an answer. He threatens to relieve you of your responsibilities and replace you with "someone who gives a damn." You give in and agree to stay. He stops threatening. (Your giving in and agreeing to stay was reinforced by the termination of threats.)

In many of the examples given on negative reinforcement, there is something else going on. Remember what I said about positive reinforcement: that something is added to the environment. Look at the above examples and see if you can identify who was being *positively* reinforced.

The kid who did the twisting and hurting was positively reinforced by you — you *gave* him the behavior he demanded.

The child who did the poking and interrupting was *given* your attention. Although you spoke impatiently, it was still attention.

Your boss *got* what he wanted from you only when he threatened you. Your agreeing to stay positively reinforced his behavior of threatening.

Unfortunately, this type of interaction is not uncommon. Most people want their lives to be pleasant and give in to others in order to achieve peace and quiet.

Each act of "giving in" is accidentally "giving" positive reinforcement for unwanted behaviors. At the same time you are learning that "All I have to do is everything everybody wants and I can have peace and quiet," you are also teaching others that they must be obnoxious in order to get what they want from you.

But negative reinforcement is not all bad. For instance, if you are sick and tired of being sick and tired, you may engage in a behavior of improving physical fitness. As you become more physically fit, the feeling of being "sick and tired" ceases.

Passive behavior often leads one to a feeling of having been "shat upon." People who have frequently found themselves being passive may take the initiative to learn to be more assertive in order to terminate that old "shat upon" feeling.

Feelings of depression, loneliness, stupidity, rejection or fear often come to an end only when you elect to engage in new behaviors. You get negatively reinforced for being active, for instance, because the uncomfortable feeling of depression subsides and is replaced with feeling good.

Think of positive and negative reinforcement this way: with positive reinforcement you get goodies (money, affection, gifts, etc.) and with negative reinforcement you get relief — something unpleasant stops. Now you are ready to do some work on your own.

Here are some examples I want you to analyze. See if you can figure out who is being positively reinforced and who is being negatively reinforced, and for what. (See the end of this exercise for answers.)

1. (Let's take another look at procrastination.) Your husband has agreed to get all the information together for income taxes. As April 15th approaches, he has yet to have anything done. You are very worried the taxes won't get done. On the evening of April 14th, you offer to help get the tax information together. You lecture your husband about the pitfalls of procrastination.

2. (And, another look at untidiness.) You asked the kids several times today to pick up their belongings and take them to their rooms. By noon, everything is just as messy as it was three hours earlier. You can't stand the mess, and you pick everything up and put it away. Later, you yell at the kids and tell them not to leave their stuff about for you to pick up.

3. (While we're at it, let's check out the kid who can't do anything right.) You ask your kid to load the dishwasher. She comes into the kitchen (you are there, too) and starts to load the dishwasher. She keeps asking you how to put in this dish, and that dish. She drops a dish and breaks it. She doesn't properly scrape the dishes, and you instruct her to remove them and scrape them all. All the while she is complaining that she will never learn and doesn't want to learn how to load the dishwasher. Finally, you've had as much as you can stand. You yell at her to get out of the kitchen and you'll do the dishes yourself. You tell her she had better do it right the next time.

4. Today is the day you told yourself you would do research for your term paper. The paper has to be done tomorrow and you worry you won't get it finished. You *wish* it were already completed. *Finally*, you go to the library and work on your research. Things go well and you no longer feel worried.

5. The lawn looks terrible, you mow it. You hate mowing the lawn.

6. You live alone and there is no one around to nag you for not doing the dishes. Since you hate to wash dishes, you let them pile up all over the kitchen. Two problems ensue — you never can find a clean dish and the kitchen smells. You decide to wash the dishes.

7. Sandy asks, "Daddy, could I go over to Lisa's house to play?" Daddy says, "No. You're gone all the time. Stay home and help your mother." Sandy laments, "I never get to do anything I want to do. You're just being mean to me. Everybody else gets to play with their friends. Boo hoo. I'm the only one who has to stay home. You're mean and unfair, Daddy. Please let me go." Well, Daddy gives in to his daughter's tearful request with a warning that she ought not expect to get her way all the time.

8. You eat too much dinner and loosen your belt .

9. Your bedroom is too warm. You open an extra window for ventilation.

10. Karen's boyfriend thinks she is too fat. Karen is satisfied with her weight, but she hates having her boyfriend nag at her each time she eats a fattening food. She gives up eating fattening foods and her boyfriend quits nagging her.

11. Whenever you and your lover quarrel, you walk out.

Answers:

1. Your husband got help at the last minute — he was reinforced putting off the tax work. Your behavior of helping with the taxes put a stop to your worrying. (By the way, your lecture affected nothing — you had already reinforced the behavior you didn't like.)

2. No reason for kids to put their stuff away. The maid (that's you) will do it. You positively reinforced the kids for leaving the room messy. A little delayed nagging is a small price for maid service.

3. You positively reinforced your daughter's incompetence and whining by presenting something pleasant — your doing the work for her. You were able to stop her annoying behavior by getting her out of the room — negative reinforcement for you. The lecture was just another opportunity to vent. It changed nothing.

4. Your behavior of doing research terminated your worrying. You were negatively reinforced.

5. It doesn't matter that you hate to mow the lawn. You did it in order to eliminate its unsightly appearance. You were negatively reinforced.

6. Two problems arise from not doing the dishes: you can never find a dish and the kitchen smells. You terminate these problems (hence, you are negatively reinforced) when you do the dishes.

7. Sandy was *not* reinforced for asking nicely for what she wanted. She was, however, positively reinforced (she got to go to friend's) for being persistent and obnoxious. Daddy was negatively reinforced by the discontinuation of Sandy's incriminations. Daddy's warning was useless — he had already taught (by reinforcing) her that she could have her way.

8. You relieve the discomfort of a tight belt. You are negatively reinforced.

9. You end the condition of "too warm" — you are negatively reinforced.

10. Karen positively reinforces her boyfriend's nagging by giving in. Karen was negatively reinforced when the nagging stopped.

11. You are negatively reinforced — you escape the unpleasant interaction of a quarrel.

Extinction

So now you know how to strengthen behaviors. But what if that is not your goal? What if you want to eliminate a behavior? Let's see if you can logically conclude one means for eliminating an unwanted behavior.

What we had before was a behavior followed by something (reinforcement). What if we had the behavior followed by *nothing*? In other words, what if we no longer reinforced the behavior? That makes sense. If reinforcement strengthens a behavior, then it seems reasonable that the complete absence of reinforcement would weaken the behavior. By George! I believe we've got it!

We have just re-invented the method of *extinction.*

Extinction is: A reduction in the rate of a behavior following the elimination of the reinforcer which previously maintained the behavior.

Or, we could say: When the behavior happens, it's followed by nothing. If the behavior is *consistently* followed by nothing, the behavior will happen less often (or not at all).

The word "consistently" gives us that element of "life is not easy." One of the reasons life is not easy is that it is hard to be consistent. If you are not able to be consistent, don't even read this section on extinction. Don't touch it with a ten foot pole unless you are 100% positive you can withhold your reinforcement 100% of the time.

For those of you who believe you can be consistent, I'll tell you why it's important.

A behavior that gets reinforced every single time is not as strong as a behavior that gets reinforced every now and then. Behaviors that get reinforced every now and then are more persistent than behaviors which are reinforced all the time. Here is what you can expect when you use extinction: *The behavior will get worse before it gets better.*

Here is what that means:

1. The behavior will get more intense (e.g., from little cries to louder ones.)

2. The behavior will vary (e.g., from crying to screaming, yelling, kicking, hitting)

3. The behavior will go on for longer than it did before (e.g., from five minutes to 15 minutes).

Remember — the behavior you are trying to eliminate is one that has been taught. It is one which was *unintentionally* reinforced. When you use extinction, you must intentionally withhold the reinforcement you formerly gave.

Also remember to look at your results, not your intentions. You may intend to set someone straight with one of your lectures, but look at your record. Let's face it. Lectures rarely achieve what you intend them to achieve.

When you decide what behavior you want to eliminate, also decide which one you want to reinforce. Don't take away an *inappropriate* attention-getting behavior without reinforcing an *appropriate* attention-getting behavior.

If an individual gets most of his attention from others for being inappropriate and you eliminate that behavior, then you eliminate his most important means of getting attention. Give the individual a new tool for getting attention.

Don't try to do everything at once. Eliminate one behavior at a time. For instance, if someone you live with pouts, throws temper tantrums, picks on you, and makes false accusations, use extinction on only one of those behaviors at a time.

There was a mother who ended up preparing special food at every meal for members of the family who did not like the main meal. She was running herself ragged to please everyone. Soon it got to the point no one wanted what she wanted to serve. Everybody wanted his own special meal. Finally she put her foot down.

She announced to her family that she would be preparing only only meal each evening. Those who did not care for what she prepared could feel free to prepare their own food. Well, as you might suppose, there was a lot of moaning and groaning. But she stood her ground. ("After all," she thought, "I've taught them they can expect to receive special meals. There's bound to be some resistance in the beginning.")

She was right. There was resistance. Some of the kids didn't even come to the dinner table. The ones who came to the dinner table complained that they all had to eat slop. But, she persisted. She did not reply to or acknowledge all the snide, derogatory comments. Whenever someone did compliment her on the meal, she graciously thanked them and told them she was glad they enjoyed her cooking. She was especially complimentary to the person who tried a new food.

Although it was really rough to handle the displeasure of her family, particularly in the beginning, she did it. She talked to herself a lot then. She would remind herself that they were using the best means they knew to get her to comply; that of course they would expect her to submit to their demands — she always had before; that if she gave in now to their demands, she would always have to; that what she wanted was every bit as important as what they wanted and she was willing to suffer some initial discomfort; that the only reason they were all getting more from her than she cared to give was that she had taught them to be persistent in their demands; and that her actions would be the only way she would teach them they could not always get what they wanted from her.

Gradually, people stopped eating peanut butter and jelly sandwiches, and started coming to the dinner table more often. She continued to compliment the behaviors she liked — that of being at the table with the family, and that of trying new foods.

Surprise! She got more than she bargained for. All she had hoped for was that she would end up cooking only one meal. What she got in addition was a pleasant family dinner hour. No more bitching about the food. No more bickering between her and her children and husband. People were actually being kind to each other.

These are the kinds of changes you can expect to get if you are consistent and persistent. If this sounds like a fairy tale to you, then it's probably because you've never experienced the success of being consistent and persistent.

Here's what she could have messed up: she could have argued back with them when they verbally attacked her; she could have failed to compliment the behaviors she liked; she could have given in "just a little, but no more"; she could have felt guilty and helped people prepare their own food; she could have worried about whether her family was eating properly and prepared snacks later in the evening; she could have been hateful and resentful for their treatment of her; she could have blamed them for being awful instead of acknowledging to herself she had unintentionally taught them to treat her that way; she could have continued to scold those who did not come to the table (and, thereby, accidentally, reinforce the behavior of not coming to the table); she could have lectured that families "ought to be pleasant to each other and appreciate what is done for them"; or she could have gone off and pouted and cried in an effort to make them feel guilty for not coming to the table.

Her decision to stand firm for what she wanted and her behaviors that backed up that decision brought her success. Her thoughts also backed up her decision. She kept telling herself all the reasons it was important to make the change.

Imagine, please, what you think she would have done if she had been thinking: "This will never work; I shouldn't have tried it. The kids are probably telling everyone what a mean mother I am; everyone will end up hating me for what I'm doing. No one cares about me, so there's no use in trying to get them to."

She probably would have acted a whole lot differently than she did had she been thinking those failure oriented thoughts. It is likely she would have felt guilty and given in to their demands. In her mind she took credit for having taught a behavior — even though she didn't like what she had taught. She, in turn, gave herself credit for having the ability to teach a behavior that she did like.

When someone has an obnoxious behavior, it is possible that the behavior is 1) reinforced by more than one person, and 2) that it is reinforcing in and of itself (intrinsically reinforcing).

Where possible, try to involve everyone (including the individual with the obnoxious behavior) in the plan to eliminate the behavior. Try to get others to agree to withhold their reinforcement, and get the "offender" to agree to this change. The offender will feel less like he is being attacked if he is involved in the plan. As a group, identify the reinforcers. What usually happens following the obnoxious behavior? Once the reinforcers have been identified, withhold them and anything similar to them. That is, all of you follow the behavior with a great big *nothing*.

If it is not possible to have a group plan, go ahead and use extinction with just yourself involved in withholding the reinforcement. The offender will soon learn that you do not reinforce the obnoxious behavior and the behavior will soon extinguish in your presence. That is, the obnoxious behavior may continue to occur when the offender is in the presence of others, but it will no longer occur in your presence.

When the person is simply "getting a charge" out of what he is doing (an intrinsically reinforcing behavior), then the withholding of your reinforcement will hardly matter. The behavior will continue to continue.

Take smoking, for example. No one needs to tell the smoker what a great job he's doing, or how wonderful it is that he knows how to smoke. The smoker smokes because the act of smoking is reinforcing.

The best plan for dealing with an intrinsically reinforcing obnoxious behavior is to 1) quit trying to give the person insight via lectures, and 2) reinforce like crazy behavior that is incompatible with the obnoxious one.

As a child, Antonia Brico, the orchestra conductor, was given piano lessons for the sole purpose of keeping her hands busy so she couldn't bite her fingernails. She couldn't bite her nails while she played the piano — the behaviors were incompatible.

Focus on the behaviors which are appropriate. Give your attention to the behaviors you like, not the ones you don't like.

And don't kid yourself. Attention is attention, whether it is for appropriate or inappropriate behaviors. You may label your spankings, lectures, and arguments "negative attention," but it doesn't matter what you call it, it can still be reinforcing.

Reinforcement is the most powerful tool you can use in teaching behaviors. It is powerful whether it is used intentionally or unintentionally. Because it is often used unintentionally behaviors which are not meant to be taught get taught.

Punishment

When unwanted behaviors are taught, people try to unteach them by using what they call "punishment." They think they are punishing a behavior because they can stop it immediately. They fail to look at the total picture — that is, that although the behavior stops immediately, it continues to occur with greater frequency. In fact, the frequency may increase and still the "punisher" continues to "punish."

The typical situation where this type of "punishment" occurs is between parent and child. What do you think is really going on in this example?

Dad and kid are in grocery store. Kid asks dad to buy him candy. Dad takes the kid firmly by the arm, shakes him a little and tells him to quit asking for candy. Kid shuts up immediately but a few minutes later repeats his request. Dad also gives a repeat performance. Kid immediately becomes quiet. This sort of thing continues for the entire time they are in the store.

What happened? Dad was immediately *negatively reinforced* (kid shut up) for his method of dealing with the problem. The kid was *positively reinforced* (he got Dad's attention) for his act. Although Dad *meant* to punish the behavior of asking for candy — he actually reinforced it.

So what is punishment, anyway? Punishment is: An event or object which follows a behavior and decreases the chances of the behavior occurring again.

Or we could say: If it didn't feel good, you probably won't do it again.

Punishment is indeed punishment when it results in a decrease or stopping of the behavior which was punished.

There are a bunch of problems associated with the use of punishment:

Here's what they are:

Problem 1: It gives the person being punished no information about the behavior desired by the punishing person. Your boss gives you a job to do — he wants you to design a form to be used in the office. You design the form and hand it to him. "No, no, no. This isn't what I want at all. Take it back and do it over; this one just won't work." So you take it and make extensive revisions and come back to him with it. "I told you before this isn't what I want," the boss snaps. "Look, Fred, I need this form done and I need it done right! Now can I depend on you to do it or do I have to give it to someone else?"

What was wrong with what you did? You don't know. What did he want instead? You don't know. In addition to your boss being hard to please, he is also inefficient. It would have saved everyone time if he had simply told what specifically was wrong, and what specifically he wanted.

Problem 2: The person being punished does not know which behavior is being punished. Since most of us don't do only one thing at a time, unless we are told specifically what we did wrong, we don't know why we are being punished.

Example: (Put yourself in Mike's shoes.) Mike was sitting on the floor. He was teasing the dog. He was making a lot of noise while the others were trying to talk, and he wasn't paying attention to what the others were saying. His father yelled at him, "Stop it, Mike!" So, Mike quit teasing the dog. His father then yelled, "Damn it, Mike! I said stop it. Now go to your room and stay there until you learn how to behave."

Do you know which behavior Mike was being punished for? Neither did Mike.

Problem 3: It tends to suppress other behaviors. This all hinges on the mood of the person who does the punishing. There is no way for those on the receiving end of punishment to know which behavior is wrong in the eyes of the punisher. Even behaviors which have been delightfully reinforced in the past can now seem wrong to the punishing person.

You call out, "Hey, Honey, can I help you with that?" Honey replies, "What's the matter, don't you think I can do anything by myself? Where do you get off thinking I can't do anything without you?" You reply, "I'm sorry. That isn't what I meant at all. I was only trying to be nice." Honey replies, "Yeah, yeah. You and your nicey, nice. Well, I'm getting tired of your nicey, nice."

Since you don't know exactly what Honey meant, it is likely you will not do *anything* that can be construed as nicey, nice. Your behaviors will be suppressed.

Problem 4: The wrong behavior gets punished. Jane comes home late one Friday night after work and Roger gets mad at her. He accuses her of not caring for him, of being out with another man, and threatens to leave her if she stays out late again. Throughout the week Roger continues to bring up her last Friday night's behavior. Although Jane was home at the regular time Tuesday through Thursday, nothing was said of that. Friday night rolls around, Jane stays out with her friends — this time later than before. She comes home, Roger goes into his act. Soon, Jane is staying late several nights a week. Roger never misses punishing her for it.

The behavior Roger intended to punish was staying out late. But staying out late increased in frequency and duration. The behaviors that were actually punished were coming home and being at home.

Problem 5: The punishing person becomes aversive. One sure way not to get punished is to avoid being around the person who does the punishing. It's no fun to be around someone who physically or verbally strikes at you. Although the punishing person *means* to teach the behavior is wrong, what he more often successfully teaches is: don't get caught doing it. There are no consequences for doing wrong if the punishing person is not present.

What happens to your driving speed on the highway when you see a highway patrolman? If you are exceeding the speed limit, chances are you slow down. Your behavior changes only when the potential punisher is visible.

In the example of Jane and Roger, Roger became aversive to Jane and she avoided him. His only control over her was punitive and it occurred at home, so she learned to avoid punishment by staying away.

Problem 6: It teaches (models) aggression. Once again this is usually a problem between parent and child. The parent falls into the "do as I say, not as I do" trap. Parent spanks his child for hitting another child. Parent says (while spanking), "You know you're not supposed to hit people. Shame on you, hurting that little boy!"

The child has eyes as well as ears. Small children learn best from watching (modeling) others. Their language capabilities are not well enough developed to process the verbal message, and, what if their language is good enough? There are two messages being given: a verbal one that says "don't" and a physical one that says "here's how." Pretty confusing.

Problem 7: It elicits aggression. She says, "Well, when are *you* going to help? Or do you expect me to do *my* share and *your* share of the work?" He quickly retorts, "If all you did was *your* share for a change, I'd be happy. One minute I stop to take a breath and you have to come right in with your zingers. A person can't have one minute's peace without you opening your big mouth." She says, "Look who's got a big mouth. Yelling so loud all the neighbors can hear. I don't know why I put up with you!"

Well, why go on? You all recognize a fight when you see one. They usually start in a manner similar to the one in this scene.

With all these problems, one wonders why punishment is still used. The fact that people tend to be more punishing than they are reinforcing is even more of a puzzlement.

One of the reasons is that the punishing person gets

immediate short-term results. He can yell "stop" and he gets "stop" right now so he doesn't look beyond the end of his nose to see that in the long run the behavior continues on in the same pattern.

Also, for most of us, punishment has been modeled as the solution to the problem. It is easier to strike back at what you don't like than it is to reinforce and strengthen a behavior you do like. Teaching new behaviors takes time — punishing behaviors is quick and easy — in the short run.

We've also been taught not to let others get by with doing things wrong or incorrectly. If you let them get by with it, it would seem that you were being permissive. Permissiveness is viewed as being bad. Punishment is seen as doing something about it. You've heard the old saying, "Do something! Even if it's wrong." Well, all too often, "doing something" is wrong!

For instance, the use of extinction is essentially "doing nothing," but it works! I'm not suggesting you be permissive, only that you be effective.

Response Cost

There's another technique that can be used to decrease a behavior. That technique is *Response Cost:* The termination of a stimulus following a behavior which *decreases* the chances of the behavior occurring again. Or, if you lose something you like every time you act a certain way, then you'll probably stop acting that way.

This means, of course, losing a reinforcer when you do something that someone else deems wrong. Even though you may agree that what you did was wrong, you may not agree to the loss of that particular reinforcer.

For instance, lovers frequently take away affection and companionship when they dislike the behavior of the other. Parents often take away their child's privileges when the child misbehaves.

The reason I don't like the use of response cost is that people misuse it. They use it to get back at someone else. Here's what can happen:

You are having a pleasant telephone conversation with your girl friend. You tell her that you are going out with a friend and won't be over to see her tonight. She hangs up!

Or, your mother tells you that if you run errands for her this week, you can keep the car at your house all next week and use it with no strings attached. You run the errands and you get the car. Your mother calls and asks you to run a couple more errands for her this week. You remind her that she agreed to let you use the car with no strings attached. Within the hour, she arrives on the bus to pick up the car. She says, "If that is the way you are going to treat me, I'm sure not going to let you use my car!"

See how nasty this can turn out. You have your reinforcer, but ZAP it gets yanked out from under you.

The thing is, response cost can be used very effectively if people play fair and square. Here's how: Father says, "Brenda, I want you home in time for dinner. If you come home by 6:00 you can watch T.V. for two hours. If you're not home on time without my calling, you don't get your dessert."

Okay. See the difference? This time the contingencies were clearly specified.

Two people can even conspire together. You both want to get the car washed and waxed on Saturday. You agree that *if* together you don't get the job done, you won't allow yourselves your regular Saturday night at the movies.

Any time a reinforcer is to be taken away, make it contingent on a certain behavior. You don't gain much in the way of interpersonal relationships if you go around yanking the rug out from under people's feet.

What's more, if someone is to have a reinforcer taken away contingent upon a behavior, let it go at that. Simply take away the reinforcer. Don't lecture, scold, argue, tantrum or anything else. The loss of the reinforcer is enough.

When/Then Rule

It's better to give than to take away. You can teach discipline by using the *When/Then Rule* (Or, as it is sometimes called, *Grandma's Rule*).

When you get your room all straightened up, then you can go outside.

When you finish your meat and vegetables, then you can have dessert.

When I get the dishes done, then I can go play tennis.

The When/Then Rule is most effective when small chunks of behavior are reinforced. It differs from the all work before play theme. All work before play means you have to do large chunks of behavior before you get any reinforcement. Better to reward small chunks.

If you have a lot of work to get done today, don't dangle one reward at the tail-end of the achievement. Tell yourself that when I have worked for one hour, I will have a coffee break for 15 minutes. I will take a lunch break when I am halfway through with my work. I will have an afternoon coffee break when I have worked another two hours.

I love this gimmick. It's a great way to get yourself going and a tricky way to keep right on going. It's also good for getting others to do work. Arrange that this much work gets done, and this much free time is earned. It's nice to have the goal of a reward to work toward.

Now that you know how to get more of what you want by being nice, I hope you will try it.

APPENDIX I

Arguments Against Irrational Thoughts

Out of the following list of arguments, you may be able to find some that you can use on your own irrational thoughts. If not, maybe these will help you think of some effective arguments for yourself.

I don't know that's true.
The evidence doesn't support this.
Even if it's true, I can handle it.
It's okay not to be perfect.
I won't know unless I try.
Others might respect me for this.
I'll feel better about myself if I try it.
It's up to me to satisfy my desires.
I have a responsibility to myself to act.
Others have rights too.
This thought will lead me to act in ways that I don't want.
I'm catastrophizing.
Thinking constructively will be more productive.
If I begin small, I can achieve more.
This is a self-defeating thought.
This will keep me from reaching my goal.
This only hurts me.
This only hurts others.
That's irrational.
That's dumb.
That's not the way I want to be.
That's the old me.
That thought is just a bad habit.
Nothing ventured, nothing gained.
My rights are important.
Their rights are important too.
I'm putting myself in this situation. It's foolish to blame others.
I'm responsible for what I think and feel; others aren't.
I can try to solve the problem. I am not stuck with it.
If I want things to change, I will have to act.
Waiting for others to meet my needs is foolish.
They don't even know what I want.
Making my desires known improves my chances of getting them fulfilled.
Giving others their rights is as important as standing up for mine.
Others have the right to say "no."

Asking for what I want is important.

My thoughts and feelings are important. It is better to express them.

Disagreeing with someone does not always lead to quarrels.

I am making an assumption about something and acting as though it is true.

I cannot read minds. I don't *know* what someone else is thinking.

Others cannot respect me if I do not respect myself.

If I don't like something, it is my responsibility to say so.

Others cannot read my mind.

I'm inventing problems for myself.

I don't have enough information to reach a logical conclusion.

Thinking this way only makes me upset needlessly.

I'm being dramatic, but I'm also being irrational.

I'm feeling sorry for myself.

Others have a right to act in their own best interest.

I have the right to act in my own best interest.

I believe what I did was right. He has a right to another opinion.

I've got to outgrow that kind of thinking.

I have a right to my time.

I've taught them to expect this of me. Now I can *unteach* it.

This thought isn't helping me to solve the problem.

I've done something similar before — I can try it again.

Trying is better than doing nothing.

Doing it this time may make it easier next time.

Failing once doesn't mean always failing.

I can learn from my mistakes.

Exaggeration only makes it worse.

Hearing the other side before I make a judgment will make a difference.

Confidence (or "assertion" or "self-esteem" etc.) builds a little at a time.

There was one aspect which was assertive.

Putting myself down doesn't help solve this issue.

Jumping to conclusions is unfair on my part.

If I keep arguing against this irrational thought, my emotions will get better.

I can't expect everyone to agree with me.

Disagreement doesn't mean rejection.

Honesty is more beneficial than hedging.

Even though this action is difficult now, I know it will benefit me in the long run.

Dwelling on the past isn't going to help my future.

There are lots of good things about myself.

I do lots of things well.
With practice it will come easily and naturally.
It takes strength to ask for help.
Asking for help shows I'm interested in solving this issue.

APPENDIX II

Self-Instructions

Here is a list of self-instructions, some of which may be applicable to your situations.

Try it.
Catch them being good.
Speak up.
Wait and get more information.
Be assertive.
Calm down.
Express yourself.
Relax.
Be positive.
Stop. Get their side of the story.
Ask for it.
Take a chance.
Reinforce.
Give others their rights.
Pay attention.
Look for solutions.
Stick to the issue.
Listen to what they have to say.
Be friendly.
Do it now.
Look 'em in the eye.
Use your big voice.
Be firm.
Think rationally.
Reinforce yourself.
Take a deep breath and relax before responding.
Accomplish the goal.
Be open.
Do what you want to do.
Exercise your rights.
Look after yourself.
Look on the bright side.
Buck up! Straighten up and fly right!
Hang in there.
Keep up the good work.
Be creative.
Prepare for success.

APPENDIX III
WORK SHEET EXAMPLES

In-Class Behavior Goals

Name _____ Session _____ Date _____

GOAL I:

REPORT I:

GOAL II:

REPORT II:

GOAL III:

REPORT III:

_____

SUCCESS STORY SHARED WITH GROUP:

_____

MY OUTSIDE GOAL FOR NEXT WEEK IS:

_____

The thing I liked *most* about today's class was:

I would like to make these suggestions:

Comments, feedback, input etc.

APPENDIX III
WORK SHEET EXAMPLES

Cognitive Exercise Homework

Name _____ Date _____

Instructions:
Spend at least five (5) minutes per day doing cognitive
exercises. Record appropriate data below.

Date	Irrational Thought	How Many Repetitions	Which Technique	Rating Before 1-10	Rating After 1-10

APPENDIX III
WORK SHEET EXAMPLES
Suggested In-Class Behavior Goals

Here are some examples of in-class goals that you will probably find helpful to you in achieving your major goal. These are designed to serve as practice situations, but they should be carried out in a sincere manner. Please select easy ones to begin with as it is important that you accomplish the task. As you go along, choose ones that are slightly more difficult.

— Ask one question of the instructor.

— Ask one question of another student.

— During group discussion, say something in response to what another student says. (Or to what the instructor says.)

— During the break, ask someone their name and one question about themselves.

— Invite someone (whom you do not already know) to join you during the break.

— Start a conversation with someone you don't know.

— Reinforce yourself to yourself (that is, covertly) three times for something you say or do.

— Non-verbally reinforce six people — tell me what you did.

— Use three different non-verbal reinforcers for at least three people — what did you do?

— Observe the behaviors of others in the group — what are three brief verbal comments made that, to you, seem reinforcing?

— Speak to or greet verbally two people.

— Introduce yourself to someone you would like to get to know better.

— Say something positive about yourself during a conversation with one or two people.

— Give eye contact and a smile to three people. Who were they?

— Ask someone their name, one question, and reinforce them once.

— Reintroduce yourself to someone you are interested in.

— Look at your own behaviors — tell me two things that you did during class or break that were assertive.

— Look at the behavior of others. What assertive behaviors did you observe?

— Greet three people — use their names.

— Use the word "I" — state a feeling.

— Use the word "I" — state an opinion.

— State at least one opinion about something being discussed or explained.

— Ask someone to elaborate on a statement or point of view.

— Start a conversation with someone and during the conversation say something positive about yourself.

— Disagree with a statement made by a class member.

Suggested In-Class Behavioral Goals: Advanced

It is now time to try some slightly more difficult behaviors for in-class goals.

Use "I" — disagree with something someone says. Do this is in the form of a statement. Be direct and non-punitive.

Get involved in at least two discussions during group.

State at least one opinion about something being discussed

Reinforce yourself covertly three times. Tell me what you say to yourself.

Ask for reinforcement from someone or everyone.

Reinforce the instructor for a specific behavior.

Say something nice about someone you know but who is not present (the others need not know the person).

Just tell about two assertive things you did during class or break.

During a conversation with someone, say something nice about another group member.

Reinforce someone for a specific behavior.

Ask someone to elaborate on a statement or point of view expressed.

Start a conversation with someone, and during the conversation say something positive about yourself.

SUGGESTED READINGS

Behavioral Self-Control
Carl E. Thoreson and Michael J. Mahoney
Holt, Reinhard & Winston

Help Yourself: A Guide to Self-Change
Jerry Schmidt
Research Press

A New Guide to Rational Living
Albert Ellis and Robert A. Harper
Wilshire Book Company

Talk Sense to Yourself
Rian McMullian and Bill Casey
Distributed by Research Press and by Institute
for Rational Living

Your Perfect Right
Robert E. Alberti and Michael L. Emmons
Impact Books

FOR PROFESSIONALS:

Cognitive and Behavior Modification
Michael J. Mahoney
Ballinger

*Imagery and Daydream Methods in Psychotherapy
and Behavior Modification*
Jerome L. Singer
Academic Press

Responsible Assertive Behavior
Arthur J. Lange and Patricia Jakubowski
Research Press

Self-Control: Power to the Person
Michael J. Mahoney and Carl E. Thoreson
Brooks/Cole